Stendhal

Titles in the series Critical Lives present the work of leading cultural figures of the modern period. Each book explores the life of the artist, writer, philosopher or architect in question and relates it to their major works.

In the same series

Stendhal

Francesco Manzini

REAKTION BOOKS

For Thomas

Published by Reaktion Books Ltd
Unit 32, Waterside
44–48 Wharf Road
London N1 7UX, UK

www.reaktionbooks.co.uk

First published 2019
Copyright © Francesco Manzini 2019

Printed and bound in Great Britain by Bell & Bain, Glasgow

A catalogue record for this book is available from the British Library

ISBN 978 1 78914 157 3

Contents

Abbreviations

AM   Stendhal, *L'Âme et la Musique*, ed. Suzel Esquier (Paris, 1999)

CG   Stendhal, *Correspondence générale*, ed. Victor Del Litto et al., 6 vols (Paris, 1997–9)

DA   Stendhal, *De l'Amour*, ed. Xavier Bourdenet (Paris, 2014)

HB   Mérimée, *H. B.*, in *Carmen et treize autres nouvelles*, ed. Pierre Josserand (Paris, 1965)

HPI   Stendhal, *Histoire de la peinture en Italie*, ed. Victor Del Litto (Paris, 1996)

N   Stendhal, *Napoléon*, ed. Catherine Mariette (Paris, 1998)

OI   Stendhal, *Oeuvres intimes*, ed. Victor Del Litto, 2 vols (Paris, 1981–2)

ORC   Stendhal, *Oeuvres romanesques complètes*, ed. Yves Ansel et al., 3 vols (Paris, 2005–13)

S   Stendhal, *Salons*, ed. Stéphane Guégan and Martine Reid (Paris, 2002)

VF   Stendhal, *Voyages en France*, ed. Victor Del Litto (Paris, 1992)

VI   Stendhal, *Voyages en Italie*, ed. Victor Del Litto (Paris, 1973)

All translations from the French are my own. Where Stendhal writes in 'Franglais', as he often does at moments of high emotion, I have preserved his English in italics, sometimes alongside a few words of French, in order the better to convey the oddity of the original.

Pierre-Joseph Dedreux-Dorcy (1789–1874), *Stendhal*, 1839, oil painting.

Introduction: Readers

Henri Beyle, more commonly referred to as Stendhal (1783–1842), inspires a great deal of loyalty in his readers, in part because he is such wonderful company, in part also because he flatters us. We are forever being made to feel as though he is offering us his friendship and his esteem, so we tend to read his work not as the strangers from another time we in fact are, but as co-opted members of what feels like an exclusive club: the closed circle of initiates referred to by Stendhal as 'the happy few', after a joke in Oliver Goldsmith's *The Vicar of Wakefield*, in its turn a reference to Shakespeare's *Henry v*. Certainly, whenever I meet a fellow Stendhalian, I immediately feel a kinship: we few, we happy few, we band of brothers, and sisters.

It seems revealing that the first major academic journal dedicated to the study of Stendhal's work should have been given the title *Stendhal Club*. Transparently, this now-defunct fellowship and its flourishing successor, the no-less-revealingly named Association des amis de Stendhal, set about recreating the ideal society prospected by Stendhal, for example in a retrospective preface to *De l'Amour* (On Love, 1822) of 1834:

> I write only for a hundred or so readers and, out of all these unfortunate, kind, charming, in no way hypocritical and in no way *moral* human beings whom I should so wish to please, there are only one or two I've actually met. (*DA*, p. 356)

Stendhal prizes warm and open communication with his privileged readers, conceived of as his friends, having learnt to hide his emotions and opinions from ordinary readers, conceived of as cold acquaintances or even potential enemies. It is for this reason that he claimed 'one must make one's choice and write either for a wide public or for the happy few. One cannot at the same time please both' (*vi*, p. 705).

Stendhal is conscious of living in what he claims to have often heard Byron refer to as '*This age of cant*' (*orc*, ii, p. 1123) – it is possible Stendhal didn't know Byron quite as well as he said he did. As a result, Stendhal suspects most of the people he meets of striking hypocritical moralizing poses in an attempt to conform to social norms and thereby procure advancement: 'they claim to be scandalized that one has dared to say this thing, dared to laugh at this other, and so on' (*orc*, ii, p. 1123). It is very tiring always to censor oneself: what a privilege it would be to speak only with the friends one esteems and to whom one can say absolutely anything without fear of being misunderstood. Hence Stendhal's concept of the 'benevolent reader' (*oi*, ii, p. 533), for whom he writes in a kind of code, for want of a more perfect expressive medium: 'There are no doubt some noble and tender souls among us who are like Mme Roland, Mlle de Lespinasse, Napoleon, the condemned man Lafargue, etc. Would that I could write in a sacred language understood by them alone!' (*vi*, p. 880) Even more than as some ideal contemporary, this benevolent reader is imagined as the reader of the future: 'I confess that the courage to write would desert me if I didn't think that one day these pages would appear in print and be read by some soul loved by me – by a being such as Mme Roland or M. Gros, the surveyor.' (*oi*, ii, p. 429) It is the unknowability of this future reader that particularly attracts Stendhal, for it is this negative quality that encourages him in his sincerity:

Not feeling up to anything, not even to writing official letters for my work, I had the fire lit and now write this, hopefully neither lying to my reader nor to myself, taking pleasure in doing so as though writing a letter to a friend. What ideas will that friend have in 1880? How different they will be to the ideas of my own time! [. . .] This is a new experience for me: conversing with people knowing neither the cast of their mind, nor the education they'll have received, nor their prejudices, nor their religion! What an incentive to tell the *truth*, the simple *truth*, for nothing else lasts. [. . .]

But one must take so many precautions if one is not to catch oneself telling lies! (*OI*, II, pp. 536–7)

Stendhal's fictions likewise set out to tell us the truth: 'The truth, the bitter truth', as the epigraph to the first book of *Le Rouge et le Noir* (The Red and the Black, 1830) would have it (*ORC*, I, p. 351). That this epigraph should falsely be attributed to the French revolutionary Danton also tells us that Stendhal's truths will often be wrapped up in lies the better to shield them from profane eyes, there, in fact, being no sacred language to convey them in their pure form. But we, his unknown friends, will understand what he is trying to say to us – recognize his sincerity – because we are noble in our sentiments, being just like Mme Roland or M. Gros, the surveyor, that is to say just like Stendhal, only different.

Stendhal's fictions deftly encourage us, their readers, to identify with their narrator and with their author: often we conflate these two personae, but they are in fact quite distinct. Even more so, his fictions encourage us to identify with their hero(in)es, for these young men and women would remain forever baffling to us were we not to learn to see the world from their peculiar perspectives. It is not uncommon for Stendhal specialists to persuade themselves, however deludedly, that they possess a unique insight into his narratives thanks to their special bond with the author and/or their incarnation of one or more of his characters (for my part, I identify with Lucien Leuwen). As a result, it feels as though Stendhal has seen the world from our perspective, and this encourages us in the hope that we might be able to see the world from his – hence, no doubt, my decision to write this biography.

There is an irony, though. In his writings, Stendhal repeatedly makes the point that he doesn't think much of academics: 'poets possess courage, whereas scholars, properly speaking, are servile and craven' (*oi*, ii, p. 759). We're the very last people likely to be able to embody one of his hero(in)es, for we're all too often male, middle-aged and middle class, which makes us highly likely also to be self-important, conformist and easily cowed. In particular, we use far too many words and never really *do* anything. Our students are much more likely to incarnate Julien Sorel or Mathilde de La Mole, especially the autodidacts among them, for they (mis)read impatiently to find out about the world, with a view one day soon to *doing* something, anything, although they know not what. Stendhal approves of unpredictable characters and unpredictable readers, drawn to extremes of behaviour and eager to replicate these in their own erratic lives, which is another way of saying that he approves of characters and readers in their late teens and early twenties. All of this also tends to mean that any middle-aged academic willing to sit down and spend a summer or two writing a scholarly biography of Stendhal is highly unlikely to be the kind of person Stendhal would have wanted to tell the story of his life. I think I can see from Stendhal's perspective sufficiently well to understand that he wouldn't have wanted me as his biographer – mind you, at least I'm Italian – preferring instead a biographer in the image of his ideal reader: 'Some young Madame Roland, the daughter of a watch engraver, secretly reading a book which she quickly hides, at the slightest sound, in one of the drawers of her father's workbench.' (*DA*, p. 69)

Anonymous artist, *Madame Roland*, 18th century, oil painting.

As you'll have noticed, Stendhal repeatedly identifies Mme Roland as his ideal reader. A leading heroine of the French Revolution, he admired her as one of the founders of the Girondin party, as herself the author of an exalted and enthusiastic set of memoirs and as a wife bolder and more intelligent than her husband, for example in her performance of many of his duties as Minister of the Interior – Stendhal's fictional wives tend mostly to be bolder and more intelligent than their husbands. In the above quotation, he alludes also to her principal literary exemplar, Jean-Jacques Rousseau, who was apprenticed as an engraver and whose father was a watchmaker. In one sense, Mme Roland is Rousseau's daughter, just as, in that same sense, Mathilde de La Mole is Mme Roland's.

One might conclude, then, that in writing for his ideal readers, Stendhal is, in fact, writing for long-dead exemplars, but actually he is writing for you: for a new generation of readers who might be thrilled and thrown off course in your own lives by the examples provided by Julien Sorel and Mathilde de La Mole in *Le Rouge et le Noir*, or by Fabrice del Dongo and Gina Sanseverina in *La Chartreuse de Parme* (The Charterhouse of Parma, 1839), or by Lucien Leuwen and Lamiel in the novels that bear their names (1834–5 and 1839–42, respectively), just as Mme Roland had been by Rousseau's example and Stendhal by Mme Roland's. We are all Rousseau's children in this sense, but perhaps a better way of looking at it is that we are all potentially the children of Julien and Mathilde, Fabrice and Gina, Lucien and Lamiel. What is finally important is the affective impact of the text: Stendhal is hoping for exalted enthusiasm from his readers, not dry scholarly engagement. The former leads to action, providing often mad reasons for actually doing something, the latter only to caution and apathy. After all, as Mathilde rightly puts it, 'What great action is not *an extreme* at the moment it is attempted? Only once it has been accomplished does it seem possible to ordinary people.' (*ORC*, I, p. 629)

André Gide notes that 'to write well about Stendhal, one would need something of his manner.'[1] Stendhal in fact wrote numerous biographies, but as an enthusiast, looking for an opportunity to share his passions and otherwise to converse sincerely with the friends among his readers. In an autobiographical fragment of 6 January 1831, he tells us that this was a task he particularly enjoyed, even though he no longer has the patience for the hard work involved (*OI*, II, p. 970). But, in reality, he probably particularly enjoyed this task precisely because he never worked that hard at it.

One of his two main approaches to writing biographies appears to have been simply to copy or otherwise appropriate extracts from existing sources: why bother redrafting what is already in the public domain? The other was to rely on his defective memory, or even to make stuff up, which comes to the same thing: isn't that what we all do when we try, however sincerely, to make sense of ourselves and others, the present and the past, particularly when conversing with our friends? As Gide was to put it in his own – often quite self-consciously Stendhalian – autobiography, we might well come closest to the truth of our own lives in our fictions.[2] He was perhaps thinking of the following passage from Stendhal's journal:

> In my youth, I wrote biographies (of Mozart, of Michelangelo) which served as kinds of histories. I regret this. The *truth* about the most important as well as the least important things seems almost impossible to establish, at least the *somewhat detailed* truth. Mme de Tracy used to say to me: 'One cannot attain to *truth* except in a novel.'
>
> Every day I see more clearly that, in all other contexts, it is a pretence. (*OI*, II, p. 198)

It was the thought of not having to do any actual research that lured Stendhal away from biography and towards autobiography:

> I no longer have the patience to find sources, weigh up contradictory testimonies, etc. I've had the idea of writing a life very well known to me in all of its incidents. Unfortunately, my subject is quite unknown to the public: that subject is me. (*OI*, II, pp. 970–71)

Stendhal was easily bored and cared very little about detail, the *somewhat detailed* truth being, in any case, unattainable. He nevertheless also frequently acknowledged that truth in fact resides precisely in the detail. Predominantly, his aim was to talk freely and exaggeratedly – that is to say, honestly – with his friends, who hopefully would laugh, and not take him too literally or take too much offence, having recognized his underlying sincerity. In other words, he mostly refused to restrict himself to what bores and hypocrites are pleased to palm off as the truth, preferring his honest fictions. But at other times, he went out of his way to establish quite limited truths as painstakingly as possible – Stendhal was always very good at holding contradictory ideas in his mind and making little or no attempt to resolve them; in this respect, he was similar to Balzac, a friend in later years and another very funny man.

Stendhal's various biographies and travel writings each contain a certain amount of inaccurate information, especially as this relates to places and dates: they often give a sense not just of fictionalization, but of systematic falsification as part of a broader deliberate strategy of misinformation, there being nothing quite so liberating as a lie – Stendhal thinks 'all of the arts are founded on a certain degree of falsehood' (*AM*, p. 119) and his conception of love similarly rests in large part on the privileging of falsehoods. Lies are useful, for without them we would be left facing only 'the bitter truth' (*ORC*, I, p. 351). Nevertheless, in his autobiographical writings, Stendhal's ostensible quest is often for 'the simple *truth*' (*OI*, II, p. 537). Thus it is that, in the *Vie de Henry Brulard* (The Life of Henry Brulard, composed in 1834–6), he sets about sketching complicated maps to establish his exact location in the course of an event he is recounting, as a means of both reliving and explaining it.

The best way to locate Henri Beyle, though, is not on a map but in Stendhal's fictions, including the fiction that is the *Vie de Henry Brulard*, his most developed (pseudo-)autobiography: Henri Beyle is to be found somewhere between Henry Brulard and Octave de Malivert (from *Armance* (1827)) and Roizand (from *Une position sociale* (A Social Position, composed in 1832–3)) and Lucien Leuwen on the one hand, and Mathilde de La Mole and Lamiel on the other, for he was none of these fictional characters, just as he was not Stendhal either, but rather all of these creations were, to varying degrees, proximate versions of himself.

To write in Stendhal's manner, as advocated by Gide, is to write in a voice that would be distinctively one's own and not to mind the inherent ridiculousness of such singular utterance; it would be not to bother saying the kinds of things that are usually said on any given topic, but instead to say other things that are personal and quite possibly odd; it would be to write with enthusiasm and sincerity, as well as generosity, by which Stendhal means taking the trouble to understand and accommodate the perspectives of others; it would be to write as though to one's friends.

Stendhal is forever reminding us that the world looks very different to different people, depending on their perspective, for instance going out of his way to make this point at length in the preface to his first novel, *Armance*. As Flaubert would eventually also say, in a near paraphrase of Stendhal, 'there is no such thing as reality, there are only ways of seeing.'[3] More generally, Stendhal organizes all his fictions around competing perspectives that produce different readings and different sets of emotions, whether female or male; young, middle-aged or old; Parisian or provincial; French, Italian or German; working class, middle class or aristocratic; imaginative or logical; idealistic or ironic; naive or cynical. In the end we are left with no definitive reading or set of emotions that we can impose on characters or events, but rather with a set of more or less appealing (mis)understandings that help us to make sense of ourselves and of our friends as much as they help us to make sense of the text itself. Nevertheless, one of the curious sensations provided by Stendhal's fictions is one of sudden apparent understanding. For example, it is never stated in the text of *Armance* that Octave de Malivert is sexually impotent, or gay, or mad, or a self-pitying Romantic – that is to say, simply deluded – but it is very easy to become convinced, as a reader, that one has made the certain discovery that he is indeed one or the other of these things. It is never stated in the text of *La Chartreuse de Parme* that Fabrice del Dongo is the biological son of the Lieutenant Robert, but arriving at this certainty was the most exciting moment of my own teenage reading life. The sensation was, and still is, one of suddenly floating through space as various narrative elements reorder themselves, suddenly to make a different and better kind of sense. But what faith, finally, can we place in these reordered narratives, however certain we might suddenly be of their truth? As Stendhal ironically puts it in his introductory remarks to *La Duchesse de Palliano* (The Duchess of Palliano, 1838), mostly the translation of an original Italian manuscript from the Renaissance:

> Literary vanity tells me that it might perhaps have been possible for me to augment the interest of certain situations by developing them further, that is to say by guessing what these characters were thinking and giving a detailed account of those thoughts to the reader. But can I, a young Frenchman, born north of Paris, really be certain of my ability to guess what an Italian soul might have felt in 1559? The most I can hope for is to guess correctly what might be considered elegant and piquant by my French readers of 1838. (*ORC*, III, p. 15)

Already in 1817, Stendhal had expressed the same idea in the *Histoire de la peinture en Italie* (A History of Italian Painting):

> When we read the chronicles and fictions of the Middle Ages with the sensibility of nineteenth-century men and women, we imagine what their protagonists must have felt, we impute to them a sensibility that would have been as impossible in them as it is natural to us. (*HPI*, p. 478)

By the same token, what certainty can we have as twenty-first-century readers that we can make sense of the ways of seeing – or understand the sensibility – of fictional young French and Italian men and women from the first half of the nineteenth century?

Our generosity may well lead us to the truth, whether simple or bitter: allow us to see the world from Julien's perspective, or Mathilde's, or Lucien's, by feeling what we perhaps correctly take to be their same emotions. It might, therefore, allow us to understand their stories more accurately and more fully, and to pass judgement on them more equitably. But generosity is also associated by Stendhal with gullibility. As readers, we may well end up imputing our own thoughts and motivations to characters who turn out to be quite differently perceived by others. What matters, however, is what we persuade ourselves to be true, for truth itself, whether simple or bitter, is as inaccessible as the God that Stendhal liked to tell his friends does not exist, which is another way of saying that all of our human truths are no more than fictions. In *De l'Amour*, for example, Stendhal focuses on the illusion of beauty (beauty as a lie) and its related illusion of happiness that together go to produce the extended exercise in delusion that is love. We can never know for certain if what we see in others is true, but the fictions we create around them tell us something that is perhaps true about ourselves.

In his second abortive attempt at a biography of Napoleon, the *Mémoires sur Napoléon* (Memoirs of Napoleon), composed in 1834–6, Stendhal explicitly abandons the concept of writing a traditional Life of his subject, noting in his preface of 1836 that 'the author is conceited enough to wish not to *imitate anybody*' (*N*, p. 245). He tells us that, if asked to describe his manner, he would compare it to that of Michel de Montaigne or that of Charles de Brosses, writers whose distinctive voices particularly excited his respect and esteem; he also describes his manner as antithetical to that of Narcisse-Achille de Salvandy, a stuffed shirt recently elevated to the Académie française, whose narcissistic voice particularly excited his contempt – in the *Vie de Henry Brulard*, Salvandy is repeatedly cited alongside Chateaubriand as a literary example to be avoided. In a note to self, written a few months later in 1837, Stendhal goes on to define his new method in more detail:

> Ordinary histories [. . .] set out a case for and against, making a great show of impartiality, in the manner of [the Roman historian] Sallust, leaving it to the reader to pronounce judgement.
>
> As a result, such judgements can only be commonplace: *X is a crook or a man of honour.* As for me, I pronounce my own judgements, and they are based on a more intimate and above all a more delicate understanding of right and wrong: the judgements of a generous soul. (*N*, p. 247)

To be generous is to make the effort to understand the perspectives of others in all their complexity: to produce multiple, sometimes contradictory judgements, and never to moralize, that is, 'lie in order to advance one's career as a writer' (*DA*, p. 340), or otherwise reduce one's subject. Some people, moralizing liars like Salvandy, don't deserve such consideration. As a stuffed shirt, he is just a waste of Stendhal's time, although Vaize, a fictional stuffed shirt, reminds Lucien Leuwen that even 'the vilest scoundrels are vain and possess a sense of honour after their own fashion' (*ORC*, II, p. 419): even a Salvandy has a point of view worth considering, if only life weren't too short. Other people, in this case Napoleon, do deserve such consideration, for they remain estimable despite their faults: they are neither in bad nor in good faith, but rather endlessly complicated and unpredictable in their thoughts and actions. 'It's that Napoleon wasn't against *all* good ideas,' Stendhal drily observes (*VI*, p. 799). Put another way, 'it is not as a follower but as a moralist that Stendhal loves Napoleon.'[4] Writing in 1836, Stendhal makes a similar point:

My aim is to reveal this extraordinary man, whom I loved while he was alive and whom I now esteem with all the contempt inspired by those who have come after him.

I believe such is the general feeling.

I make no claim to writing the history of France from 1794 to 1815 and I shall speak as little as possible of general historical events. (*N*, p. 249)

Esteem matters to Stendhal: 'I fear only those I esteem' (*DA*, p. 337), he once revealed in a footnote, by which he, in part, meant that the first step on the path to freedom is not to care about the opinions of stuffed shirts – that is, 'papier-mâché souls' or 'souls of mud', to use Stendhal's own habitual idioms: 'The contempt of those I find contemptible is a matter of indifference to me' (*s*, p. 57). Quite. The corollary is that we should very much care about the opinions of the happy few we do in fact esteem, hence the fear they inspire, for 'in others, we can only esteem ourselves' (*HPI*, p. 235) and so, when those we esteem do not esteem us, it is as though we were discovering our own contempt for ourselves. Stendhal had met Napoleon – it is possible he did not know Napoleon quite as well as he said he did. He esteemed him personally as an 'ardent soul' (*N*, p. 285).

As far as Stendhal was concerned, Napoleon sometimes made decisions squalidly in his self-interest – of course he did, what political leader doesn't? – but also sometimes disinterestedly for the benefit of the French nation, all to the best of his ability and informed by an ever-changing set of partial perspectives. 'For,' as Napoleon himself asks, 'what is a man once he no longer esteems himself?' (*N*, p. 548). Stendhal thinks his memoir will be worth something thanks to the delicacy with which he will make sense of Napoleon's perspectives and also on account of what he refers to as the 'unaffected originality' of his own manner: 'if I had to censor myself, I wouldn't have the patience to keep going' (*N*, p. 247). To save time, Stendhal intended the bulk of his biography to be made up of extracts culled from other books. In the end, he did not have the patience to keep going.

This biography will not copy from other books, but it will be as personal and as sincere and as generous as I can make it. Other biographies of Stendhal set out the known facts, exhaustively and exhaustingly. If you want to find out where Stendhal was on any given day, or which woman he may or may not have been in the process of pursuing at that particular moment in time, there are better books for you to consult. But if you want an intimate and intricate personal account of Stendhal's changing perspectives on the world, then hopefully you will have the patience to keep reading – I shall think of you as a friend.

1

Names and Identities, 1783–90

Stendhal ends a very brief start at an autobiography, written in 1831, with the words 'I was born in Grenoble on 23 January 1783 [. . .]' (*OI*, II, p. 971). Perhaps discouraged by the pedantic accuracy of this date, he promptly gives up on the notion of completing either this sentence or the story of his life – none of his autobiographies are finished in any conventional sense, although the others are admittedly all considerably more developed than this one. The 'I' is in any case misleading: Stendhal rarely wrote in his own name except administratively, perhaps in some small part because his own name was not in fact his own, but rather that of his elder brother, the first Henri Beyle, who had been born almost exactly a year earlier, on 16 January 1782, only to die a few difficult days of life later. No doubt the second Henri Beyle was both conceived and conceived of as a consolation to his still grieving parents. From an early age, however, he appears to have become adept at frustrating their expectations, at least if the account of Stendhal, or rather Henry Brulard, his (pseudo-)autobiographical avatar, is to be believed – there may in fact be little reason to believe either of them.

Stendhal appears to have identified with the name Henri – he was in fact christened Marie-Henri – but seems to have preferred it in its foreign versions: the English Henry of the *Vie de Henry Brulard* and the Italian forms, Arrigo and Enrico, which he used in two projected epitaphs for his imagined tombstone. It was important to him to rewrite his first name: to customize it by stretching it to encompass all the many people and nationalities he had become by dint of living, writing and loving, the three activities by which he further defines himself in the epitaphs.

Stendhal appears to have been less fond of his surname, as indicated by his obsessive use of pseudonyms. As far as we can tell, his main objection to the name Beyle – pronounced and sometimes wrongly transcribed as 'Belle' – was to its status as a patronym. From an early age, Henry Brulard claims he equated paternity with tyranny, which is perhaps in part why Henri Beyle never went on to have children of his own. He likewise considered the institution of marriage to function as a male tyranny over women, which is perhaps why he never went on to marry – although he did propose to a sequence of women, interestingly none of whom he loved as much as the women to whom he did not propose and all of whom very sensibly turned him down. Brulard concludes that it was probably just as well that he had never been accepted, noting that 'happiness for me is to give no orders to anyone and to take none in my turn' (*oi*, ii, p. 948) – that is, happiness is finally freedom, even more than it is love. If Henry Brulard lists love as 'always my chief, or rather my only preoccupation' (*oi*, ii, p. 767), it is because, as a Romantic, he hoped one day to find a love that might, however improbably, take the form of a perfect coincidence of two freedoms.

Oddly, Stendhal never switched to the matronym Gagnon, associated with his beloved mother Henriette, his beloved maternal grandfather Henri and his beloved maternal great-aunt Élisabeth. Instead, he generated hundreds of often extremely silly pseudonyms: estimates vary between 170 and 350. He eventually settled on (Baron Frédéric de) Stendhal as his principal, but by no means exclusive, pen name and Dominique – after Domenico Cimarosa, the composer of his favourite opera, *Il matrimonio segreto* (The Clandestine Marriage, 1792) – as his pet name for himself.

Stendhal's choice of pen name may have been intended as a nod in the direction of the writer Mme de Staël, traditionally pronounced

'Stahl' – we think we know that Stendhal ought to be pronounced to rhyme not only with 'Stahl' but with the French word *scandale*, on the strength of his occasional use of the verb *stendhaliser* as a pun on *scandaliser*, although there is in fact some dispute about how *scandaliser* was pronounced in the first half of the nineteenth century, so actually we don't really know at all.

The name appears to have been derived from that of Stendal, a town in Brandenburg: the totemic 'h' for Henri/Henry may have been inserted also to make the name appear more barbarously Teutonic. As we shall see, Stendhal spent part of the Napoleonic period as an administrator in Germany, and perhaps he chose to adopt the name of a place he had passed through for personal reasons that are now mysterious. Or he may have been attracted to the name of the town on account of its having been the birthplace of the art historian Johann Joachim Winckelmann.

Stendhal may have been particularly drawn to Winckelmann by the latter's murder in Italy (Stendhal was always very interested in murders) or status as Europe's foremost expert on art (Stendhal was, by then, trying to launch himself as an expert on Italian painting) or homosexuality, as evidence of his singularity. Stendhal may even obliquely have been signalling his own (latent? active?) bisexuality: his friend Prosper Mérimée reports that Stendhal used to insist that all the great men of history were attracted to their own sex, citing Jesus Christ and Napoleon as examples (*HB*, p. 446).

It is not clear whether Stendhal ever really considered himself to be a great man – in this respect, he appears more modest than Balzac, who likewise associated homosexuality with superior singularity, most notably in the recurring character of Vautrin, and for whom his own greatness was never in any serious doubt. It is similarly not clear whether Stendhal was sexually drawn to men, although on occasion he does record himself to have been captivated by male beauty. What does seem certain is that he found the idea of both male and female homosexuality at once unsurprising and charming; that many of his friendships were intense, including some with men; and that he experienced friendship – the giving and receiving of esteem – as a form of love. We shall never know if Stendhal ever slept with a man, although the balance of probabilities is that he didn't, any more than we shall ever know whether, in *Armance*, Octave de Malivert is gay, sexually impotent, mad or a Romantic. Possibly Octave is latently or intermittently or indeterminately all of those things; possibly Stendhal was too. To think one has found something out about Stendhal or one of his fictional characters is typically to miss lots of other things entirely.

The artist formerly known as Marie-Henri Beyle produced an endless series of false identities, some of which he wrote about and have therefore been preserved. He appears to have had the thought that these multiple selves might successively, cumulatively and contradictorily reflect – and ultimately even constitute – his real self, increasingly divergent from the self he was born to inhabit: the self that was to have been determined by parental expectations, already formed around his dead namesake elder brother, and by his inherited identity as a middle-class provincial Frenchman.

Stendhal ought really to have stayed all his life in Grenoble and become a lawyer, following in the footsteps of his father, Chérubin Beyle, who had in fact inherited his office at a relatively young age from his own lawyer father. The French Revolution appears to have encouraged Stendhal in the thought that his life could depart radically from these and other expectations, for he conceived of the Revolution as an enabler of radical personal freedom, including his cherished freedoms to redefine and reinvent himself – hence his endless choices not just of new names and personae, but of new and changing civic and national identities.

If Stendhal used his imagination to write, unwrite and rewrite an ever-changing set of selves, it was in order the better to tend towards his real self. Curiously, however, the move away from his origins brought him full circle back to his patronym. The name Beyle resurfaces in *beylisme*, a word Stendhal coined in 1811 to describe his practice of defending his real self against normative external attack, most notably by rejecting the false ideas of conventional morality; it resurfaces again in the epitaphs Stendhal composed for his tombstone, in which he appears as Arrigo Beyle and Enrico Beyle. Thus at those moments when he sought most rigorously to account for what he truly was, and what he truly had been, Stendhal appears to have accepted that he was still in part the product of his patriarchal family.

There is always a tension in Stendhal between things as he would like them to be and things as they are, between the ideal and the real. The truth, at any given point in time, is probably a combination of the two, for we are always more than what we rationally appear to be, in Stendhal's case, more than simply Henri Beyle from Grenoble, but less than what we would imaginatively wish to be – less than Arrigo Beyle from Milan.

All this talk of 'real' selves must sound terribly naive – happily, Stendhal is always at least one step ahead. At the centre of each of us, Stendhal gives every impression of thinking, is a void around which orbit acquired fragments of personality. His two main autobiographical projects turn around the questions of what kind of person he might have been and what value that person might have possessed – what the orbiting fragments add up to, if anything. Lucien Leuwen likewise asks himself, and finally others – his father, a friend – whether he has any value. But Stendhal understood that asking other people was typically of little use, for we are likely to be perceived very differently by each of the friends, acquaintances or enemies who come to behold us. Even more radically, Stendhal came to understand that this 'real' self was in fact particularly unknowable to himself. As Henry Brulard puts it, 'what eye can see itself?' (*VHB*, II, p. 535). So should we just give up trying to know ourselves? No: Stendhal found two answers to his problem. The people we most esteem are those who can most be trusted to know us and indeed to tell us what our true value might be – hence the fear they inspire. Also, we are the sum of our performances of ourselves. This idea of performance as the closest we might be able to come to representing ourselves accurately, or our fictions of the self as the closest we might be able to come to the truth of ourselves, is part of what helps us to make sense not just of Stendhal but also of such intensely histrionic heroines as Mina de Vanghel, Vanina Vanini, Mathilde de La Mole and Lamiel – the freest, most *beyliste* and therefore, in some important ways, most appealing of his fictional characters. In the modern world emerging after the definitive fall of Napoleon in 1815, Stendhal tells us that people – especially men and even more especially French men – take themselves far too seriously: they conform to a socially imposed idea of their own dignity and live in fear of giving rise to ridicule by departing from the expectations that surround and define their socially allotted roles. Yet, for Stendhal, it is our refusal to meet such expectations that alone gives expression to the self. It is for this reason that we should find our escape by playing inappropriate roles or, even better, by appropriating roles inappropriately. It is when we seem least the person we ought to be that we are in fact most ourselves – not so much our 'real' selves as our singular selves, that is to say our own creations. As Gide once again suggestively puts it when defining what he refers to as the 'inverted sincerity (of the artist)',

> He ought not to tell the story of the life he has lived but rather to live the story of the life he will write. Put another way, let the self-portrait that is his life conform to the ideal self-portrait he would wish to see; or, put more simply still: let him be as he wants himself to be.[1]

Stendhal's surviving correspondence gives a strong indication that a number of his friends did indeed learn to understand and appreciate him, making sense of his inappropriateness by laughing as opposed to taking offence. Unfortunately, the principal extended account of Stendhal written by a friend, *H. B.* (1850) by Mérimée, although rich in suggestive anecdotes, chooses to stress the inconsistency of its subject's character and the changeability of his opinions as though such flightiness were a bad thing. If we are to judge by *Le Rouge et le Noir*, Stendhal particularly valued the unintelligibility and unpredictability of others: what he terms their singularity. Likewise, Henri Beyle valued his own unintelligibility and unpredictability, both to himself and to the people who nominally knew him best. *H. B.* in fact tells us more about Mérimée, and about how Henri Beyle played up to and parodied his friend's idea of him – for Stendhal was a staggeringly perceptive man who made a lot of jokes simply for his own amusement – than it tells us about its ostensible subject. In order to make sense of Stendhal, we need to generously acknowledge his inconsistency not as something to be resolved but rather to be enjoyed. In other words, we need to recognize what John Keats, quite separately from Stendhal and unbeknownst to him, refers to as negative capability – 'that is when man is capable of being in uncertainties, mysteries, doubts, without any irritable reaching after fact and reason'.[2]

Looking back at his childhood, Henry Brulard irritably reaches after fact and reason, even as Stendhal remains aware that everything is mystery and doubt. The story concocted by Henry is unnaturally consistent, partial and unfair. It positions him between two families: the real family made up of the various extant Beyles and Gagnons, and the ideal family that was the French Republic. In the process, it provides him with two imagined identities: Henry the downtrodden slave and Henry the precocious freedom fighter. Yet much is also revealed that does not fit either of these narratives – it is possible his

Anonymous artist, *Dr Henri Gagnon*, 18th century, oil painting.

family circumstances were not quite as grimly conflictual as he said they were.

Stendhal's early childhood was almost certainly unremarkable. He appears to have loved his mother a great deal and clung to her: Henry observes that, still a small child, he loved her the way he would one day love Alberthe de Rubempré – of whom more later – and that he would have wanted to kiss her body all over, there being no clothes to come between them (*OI*, II, p. 556); he also fairly clearly wanted his father – to whom, in later years, he would habitually refer to as 'the Bastard' – dead. Henri may have been largely unembarrassed by his infant sexuality, his mother possibly less so. That said, there is no sense of her having either encouraged or, in any hurtful way, rejected him, and probably she doted on him, despite or perhaps particularly because he passed for a relatively ugly and uningratiating child.

Henriette is described by Brulard as beautiful, graceful like a doe, kind and cultured: she even spoke Italian, reading Dante in the original. He concedes that she might have been a bit too short, but otherwise can think of no flaws in her. In particular, Brulard comes to the conclusion that she displayed two notable moral qualities: 'Henriette Gagnon was possessed of a generous and headstrong nature; I worked this out in retrospect' (*OI*, II, p. 973). Her husband – the withered, careworn and in no way cherubic Chérubin – had made something of his career as a lawyer and prospered, owning an apartment in Grenoble and a small country residence in the nearby village of Claix. Just around the corner from the Beyles, overlooking Place Grenette, one of Grenoble's main squares, lived Henri Gagnon, Henriette's doctor father.

He had once been on a pilgrimage to visit Voltaire in Ferney, as commemorated by his proud ownership of a bust of the great man, and had been part of the delegation that had welcomed Rousseau at the gates of Grenoble when the latter came to visit the city in 1768: unsurprisingly, Dr Gagnon possessed a certain social standing, both before and during the Revolution. As befitted a man of his status, he wore a powdered wig.

He appears to have been a kindly man, indulgent to his extended family, eager, whenever possible, to avoid conflict, including by sometimes (not) shielding his grandson from the consequences of his own behaviour. In his professional life, he showed himself willing to administer not only to the wealthy but to the poor, sometimes even pro bono. Dr Gagnon's sister, Élisabeth, appears, by contrast, to have possessed inflexible moral courage and, consequently, to have been quite difficult. In particular, Élisabeth had a code of honour, grandly associated both by her and by Henry with the values immortalized in Pierre Corneille's *Le Cid* (1637), to which she adhered, at whatever personal or human cost. Élisabeth was the first of many difficult women whom Stendhal would come to adore – it's possible women aren't 'difficult', but instead more likely, in a patriarchy, jealously to guard their autonomy. Henry Brulard tells us that Dr Gagnon 'esteemed and feared his sister' (*OI*, II, p. 591).

Dr Gagnon's flat, now the Musée Stendhal, was larger than that of Chérubin Beyle, lighter and more airy, as well as possessed of a terrace adorned by a trellis. It lay between Place Grenette and the public gardens, and was therefore much better situated than the parental home. Throughout his childhood, Stendhal unsurprisingly liked playing and studying there rather than in his father's flat, also because he preferred the society of his mother's family, with one exception: his aunt Séraphie. Henri came to detest his mother's sister, just as he came to detest his own sister Zénaïde – he (thought he) adored his other sister Pauline; another sister, Marie-Caroline, had died in infancy. His very strong reaction against Séraphie is no doubt connected to the event that, in Brulard's account, marked the start of Henry's moral life, shaping his sense of self evermore. When he was only seven, on 23 November 1790, Henriette died in childbirth, allegedly with Henry's name on her lips (*OI*, II, p. 973). In a curious note designed to confuse the police, Stendhal identifies himself as the widower of Charlotte Corday, another of his Revolutionary heroines (*OI*, II, p. 961): certainly Henry came to adore Charlotte, a difficult woman if ever there was one, but the note carries the trace of another, earlier bereavement. All his life after the age of seven, one of Stendhal's many identities was that of his mother's widower.

Photograph of the trellis at the side of Dr Gagnon's flat, seen from the public gardens, late 19th–early 20th century.

From the young Stendhal's perspective, Henriette had presumably been murdered by her husband twice over: first, he had, unspeakably, once again impregnated her; second, to deliver her of their importunate child, he had stupidly hired an incompetent doctor, instead of the competent doctor who would doubtless have saved her. Brulard, writing past the age of fifty, eventually concedes that his father was overcome by grief at the death of his wife, and that the marks of this grief went largely unrecognized by the young Henry: '[My mother's] room was left locked for ten years after her death . . . Now that I think of it, this sentiment on the part of my father does him a great deal of credit in my eyes' (*oi*, ii, pp. 557–8). Put more characteristically and on the face of it less charitably: 'My father, who adored his wife all the more

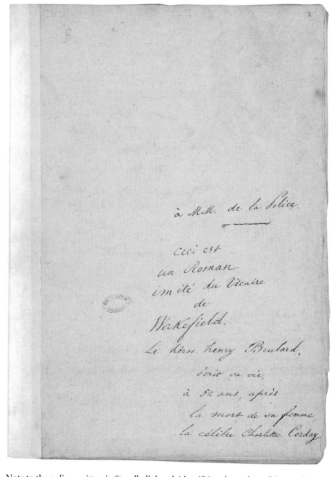

à MM. de la Police.

Ceci est
un Roman
imité du Vicaire
de
Wakefield.

Le héros henry Brulard,

écrit sa vie,
à 52 ans, après
la mort de sa femme
la célèbre Charlotte Corday.

Note to the police, written in Stendhal's hand, identifying the author of the *Vie de Henry Brulard* as Charlotte Corday's widower.

because she did not love him, was made stupid by grief. This state lasted five or six years; he started to pull himself out of it by studying chemistry first in Macquer, then in Fourcroy' (*oi*, II, pp. 973–4).

Actually, nothing could be more movingly Stendhalian than to love a woman who does not return that love and to pull oneself out of the resulting state of emotional prostration by developing an abstract passion for chemistry. The *Vie de Henry Brulard* tells us that Henriette died at the age of either 28 or thirty (*oi*, II, p. 556); in fact, she died at 33 (*oi*, II, p. 973). Numbers mattered to Stendhal, and Henry's miscalculation is no error: what he's saying is what he goes on to say explicitly, namely that his mother died 'in the flower of her youth and beauty' (*oi*, II, p. 556); what he is also saying is that she died at the age Stendhal associated with Métilde Dembowski, also of whom more later. In *De l'Amour*, Stendhal argues that young women of eighteen – the women he would go on to write about with such evident admiration in his fictions, most notably Mathilde de La Mole and Lamiel – eventually turn 28. They grow up even as they are still young, suddenly becoming capable of passion (*DA*, p. 75). Put another way, the self-assertion and the pride and the impatience he so values – his mother's quality of decisiveness – come to be tempered by generosity. Something of this process is captured in *Le Rouge et le Noir* by Mathilde's development from metaphorical princess to metaphorical queen.

Rousseau tells us in *Les Confessions* – a self-conscious model for the *Vie de Henry Brulard*, just as both *Les Confessions* and *Vie de Henry Brulard* became self-conscious models for Gide's *Si le grain ne meurt* (If It Die, 1926) – that he eventually embarked on an affair with an older woman, his aristocratic patroness, Mme de Warens. Artlessly, he tells us that his private name for her was 'Maman'. Similarly, Stendhal invests his two most developed 'angelic', as opposed to 'Amazonian' female characters, Louise de Rênal in *Le Rouge et le Noir* and Bathilde de Chasteller in *Lucien Leuwen*, with

Anonymous artist, *Caroline-Zénaïde Beyle*, 19th century, oil painting.

an almost limitless materno-erotic charge. The two categories of 'angelic' and 'Amazonian' female protagonists were first proposed by Jean Prévost, probably the most Stendhalian of Stendhal specialists, finding his death as he did in 1944, fighting for the French Resistance in Sassenage, a village near Grenoble that Stendhal knew well. Both Louise and Bathilde

Anonymous artist, *Pauline Beyle*, 19th century, oil painting.

are 28, and their stories come to be dominated by their (possible) status as mothers. For his part Rousseau had of course never known his mother: she was a figure of fantasy, intimately bound up with his guilt at having killed her. Stendhal, on the other hand, knew his mother and gave himself over to the pleasure of finding her again in his fictions.

All that said, what Stendhal most wanted was a sister. To recap, he ended up with two of them, his third having died in infancy. We shall never know whether Zénaïde was indeed the ghastly tell-tale he made out, but we do know that Pauline was both the sister he had always wanted, and not.

His side of the extensive correspondence between them has, to a large extent, survived: Henri was a very attentive brother, one might even say overbearing. From the outset, he wished her to be free and unconventional. He also saw that, as a woman in the nineteenth century, for her to have chosen such a life would have been to expose herself to great risk. The strategy he therefore advocated was one of public compliance and personal freedom. He appears to have hoped that Pauline would become not unlike Louise de Rênal, detached from her eventual husband by her inalienable pride as a free human being. Pauline duly married François Périer-Lagrange, like M. de Rênal a dull provincial obsessed with his estates, on 25 May 1808. When this husband eventually died, Pauline came briefly to live with her ostensibly loving brother, as he recalls in the *Souvenirs d'égotisme* (Memoirs of an Egotist), composed in 1832:

> I was severely punished for advising one of my sisters to
> come to Milan with me in 1816, I believe [in 1817]. Mme
> Périer attached herself to me like an oyster, charging me with
> everlasting responsibility for her fate. Mme Périer possessed
> all the virtues, as well as a fair quantity of reason and charm.
> I was obliged to quarrel with her in order to rid myself of this
> oyster, maddeningly attached to the hull of my vessel, who,
> whether I liked it or not, held me responsible for all her future
> happiness. The horror of it! (*OI*, II, p. 488)

He had dutifully written for years with unsolicited advice. What more could now be expected from him? I think it is possible that Stendhal was, finally, a not very good brother to Pauline.

It is hard to make sense of the devastation produced by the loss of his mother simply by reading Brulard's analysis of it, for this employs some of the rhetoric found in Rousseau's account of the death of his mother in *Les Confessions* (1781–8). One way to make sense of oneself, as far as both Stendhal and, after him, Gide are concerned, is to identify with the story of another. Stepping back from Brulard's own representation of the event, however, we can quite clearly see its consequences in the account of his subsequent childhood.

Henry withdrew from his family and from other children; he quickly became, and long remained, extremely angry, especially at his father, but also at his aunt, who somehow failed to understand that he had been too devastated to show overt grief: 'I had been unable to cry after the death of my mother. I only started being able to do so more than a year later, alone, at night, in my bed' (*OI*, II, p. 676). Hence, no doubt, her cruelty to him in the immediate aftermath:

> When I entered the drawing room and saw the coffin draped in black cloth *which contained my mother*, I was seized by the most violent despair: finally I understood what death was. My aunt Séraphie had already accused me of not caring. (*OI*, II, p. 567)

An unfortunate intervention by the Abbé Rey, a family friend attempting to console the grief-stricken Chérubin, had the effect of making Henry extremely angry also at Providence: '"My friend, this comes from God", he eventually said; this phrase, spoken by a man I hated to another I couldn't stand, gave me a great deal to ponder.' (*OI*, II, p. 564) 'God's only excuse is that he doesn't exist' became one of Stendhal's favourite dicta according to Mérimée (*HB*, p. 445) – Nietzsche would eventually ask himself whether he might not in fact be 'envious of Stendhal' for taking away from him 'the best atheistical joke that precisely I might have made'.[3]

Another of Stendhal's identities was therefore that of the anti-clerical atheist, although he came to like a number of perfectly estimable priests and to find sincere religious faith rather touching, not least because it struck him as evidently mad and therefore singular. More generally, Stendhal appears to have thought of madness as an exception to the prevailing hypocrisy typically encouraged by (Jesuitical) Catholicism, understanding it as a pressing need for sincere utterance, likely to make us appear ridiculous and to isolate us, but also capable of suddenly opening up unexpected paths to all-too-rare direct and urgent communication. It is possible that Stendhal was sometimes guilty of producing communication that was both too direct and too urgent, even for the tastes of the people he most esteemed.

To return to the impact of his mother's death, Henry went overnight from being a happy child to an unhappy child, and someone had to be held responsible for this numbingly awful change. It has been argued that Henry's anger reveals that he in fact considered himself to be to blame, on some level, for Henriette's death, having resented the impending arrival of a sibling and hoped that the birth would go wrong in some way.[4] Maybe. But what's perhaps more important is that Henry himself identified his moral life as starting not in fact with the death of his mother, but with the uncontrollable anger to which her sudden death gave rise.

Throughout his life, Stendhal arrived at distinctive moral positions that struck many people as immoral due to being unconventional, needlessly provocative or even pitiless. Each of these derived from intense surges of anger provoked by the endless spectacle of human injustice. Henry would frequently come to be identified as 'atrocious', an epithet first applied to him by his aunt Séraphie; he in fact claims the label as a badge of honour, we might even say as another identity. For to pass for atrocious in the age of cant is to refuse the atrocity of an unjust world. It is possible we should all be a lot more angry; equally, Stendhal argues we should all learn to laugh more at events we can't control, avoiding what he refers to as impotent hatred. Stendhal spent most of his adult life keeping these two contradictory thoughts in his head, as ever unresolved.

The new Henry, mere days into his moral life, started to think of himself as different to those around him: misunderstood, nobler, finer in feeling. Quickly, Henry became a heroic figure in his own mind: atrocious, ferocious, intransigent. This intransigence belonged at once to another age – the time of the ancients described by Plutarch in the *Parallel Lives* – and to the new age of Revolution. A further Stendhalian identity is therefore Greek and Roman: Henry as the heir to Dion, Timoleon and Marcus Brutus, Plutarch's fearless tyrannicides; or, in new money, Henry as Charlotte Corday's widower, for she had stabbed Marat in his bath under the influence of Plutarch's heroes, feverishly thumbing through her copy of the *Parallel Lives* the day before the assassination.

Élisabeth Gagnon cannot have helped her great-nephew recover from these delusions: stern, inflexible, she provided a constant reminder that one could indeed cut an isolated, heroic figure more or less indefinitely. She further encouraged Henry to start to assume yet another of his lasting identities: perhaps also remembering his mother's facility with the Italian language, and its happy musicality, Henry began to imagine himself descended not from the local peasantry but from glamorous Italians. Élisabeth's tales of her forebears led him to decide that the Gagnons hailed originally from Rome: in the sixteenth century, one of Stendhal's two favourite periods of history, the other being the extended parenthesis in his own life provided by the French Republic and Empire, a certain Guadagni or Guadaniamo murdered someone in Rome and fled the city for Papal Avignon. In reality, the entire fantasy rests only on the Gagnons having found their way to Grenoble from Provence. For Freud, such reimaginings of one's antecedents betray the neurosis associated with his concept of the 'family romance';[5] for Stendhal, they exemplify a drive for happiness, that is, freedom.

Stendhal's epitaphs for himself define him retrospectively neither as Grenoblois (perish the thought), nor as Parisian (even though most successful French men and women eventually come to identify themselves as Parisian), nor even as Roman (despite his alleged ancestor the assassin), but instead as Milanese. Even though Stendhal's German pseudonym has come to stand in for Henri Beyle's real name in the eyes of his readers, in his own eyes his life was in fact that of a Franco-Italian hybrid: Arrigo Beyle, *milanese*. The hybridity is often neglected: it is easy to assume that, by proclaiming himself Milanese, Stendhal is electing an exclusively Italian identity. But this is to forget that, even as Stendhal privileged his Italian (and German) imagination, so he remained stubbornly attached to what he considered to be his French logic: 'la LO— GIQUE' is how Mérimée tells us he pronounced the word, with a marked interval between the syllables for extra emphasis (*HB*, p. 445). As we shall see, from his childhood onwards, Henri Beyle adored mathematics, thinking of it as exempt from hypocrisy: as a pure expression of truth in an age of cant defined by lies. Over the course of his life, he developed a list of other things exempt from hypocrisy: rote memory, physical courage, winning a battle as a general, making someone laugh in conversation – you cannot pretend to be funny; you either are or you aren't. But mathematics always functioned as the touchstone for Stendhal's version of logic, just as opera and other vocal music, even more than literature, always functioned as the touchstone for his version of imagination. Nevertheless, we can also say that Stendhal developed a general interest in another manifestation of logic, namely philosophy, not in its 'mystical' German forms – in reality, he was dismissive of German philosophy for the excellent reason that he had read barely any – but in its French post-Enlightenment guise of Ideology, defined by Stendhal as the dispassionate study of how we arrive at our ideas. One of the leading lights of this movement, Antoine-Louis-Claude Destutt de Tracy, comte de Tracy, was to become Stendhal's somewhat boggled friend in 1817, having long already been his teacher thanks to his published writings, most notably the seventeen volumes of his *Éléments d'idéologie* (Elements of Ideology, 1802–15).

Destutt, and then eventually the moral squalor of post-1815 France, disposed Stendhal to try to see what Voltaire terms 'things as they are' – in *L'Ingénu* (1767), Voltaire describes his hero very

André Louis Victor Texier (1777–1864), after Charles Toussaint Labadye (1771–1798), *Antoine Destutt de Tracy*, *c*. 1789, line engraving.

much the way Stendhal liked to see himself: 'He saw things as they are, whereas the ideas we are given in our childhood make us spend all of our lives seeing things as they are not.'[6] Italy, by contrast, served as the land of beauty and imagination, a stage set for opera, showing us glimpses of things as one would wish them to be – lies. Lurking within Stendhal, from his childhood onwards, was this tension, between Voltaire and Rousseau, mathematics and fiction, logic and imagination, truth and lies, Henri/Henry and Arrigo/Enrico. It was a tension that Stendhal chose to leave unresolved. He wanted many names for himself, and many identities, the better to live in the gaps between each of these, so as to be happy, so as to be free.

2
Revolt, 1790–95

Still furiously angry at his mother's death, Henry Brulard uses his account of his childhood to present his young self as a rebel, even in infancy. Two of his earliest memories are of angering his family: by biting the proffered cheek of a cousin, Mme Marie-Louise Pison du Galland, who had demanded, and naively been expecting, a kiss; and by dropping a pair of scissors from a first-floor window onto a neighbour, Mme Benoîte Chenevaz. Plainly, at about the ages of three and four when, respectively, he perpetrated these two outrages, Henry had precious little idea what he was doing, and neither act tells us anything at all about either his innate or his acquired moral character. This, however, seems not to have been the perception of his family, and in particular of the allegedly malevolent Séraphie, whom we are told responded to the latter act by promptly accusing Henry of attempted murder. It was on the strength of these two crimes that Henry was first identified as 'a monster' (*OI*, II, p. 551) and 'atrocious' (*OI*, II, p. 551; p. 552) by his aunt. Brulard dates the start of his moral life not just to his mother's death, therefore, but to these incidents, or rather to the burning sense of renewed injustice they provoked in him. Again, Henry is following the example provided by Rousseau, for *Les Confessions* date the start of Jean-Jacques's moral life not just to the death of his mother, but to his burning sense of injustice at being falsely accused of breaking a comb. 'I revolted,' Henry notes of his four-year-old self (*OI*, II, p. 552).

Yet Brulard deliberately plays up to the image of him projected by Séraphie: he seems to congratulate himself on refusing to meet the soppy expectations of Mme Pison du Galland, for to frustrate expectations is to make oneself free; and on trying to do away with his neighbour, not least because she went on to become the mother of a particularly ghastly stuffed shirt (the absurdly named Candide Chenevaz, who eventually proceeded iniquitously to exercise the functions of magistrate in Restoration Grenoble). The infant Henry was already a tyrannicide, as though in anticipation of the Revolution to come: these incidents do, after all, so Henry hopes, say something about either his innate or his acquired moral character – no, they don't.

It is the imputation of atrocity by his pestilential aunt that appears to have prompted the young Henry to go about acquiring a range of ever more shocking opinions, seemingly as deliberate affronts to the conservative values and monarchist sympathies of his family, especially his father and aunt. If they wanted a monster, a monster is what they were going to get. In adulthood, Stendhal similarly took childish pleasure in shocking the salons of Paris with his outrageous views, seemingly as his way of compensating for the shyness that never left him, but also because he viewed all normative nineteenth-century morality as hypocritical cant to be fearlessly challenged.

At the age of five, Henry took advantage of the view from his grandfather's flat overlooking Place Grenette allegedly to witness the 'Day of Tiles' – a riot in protest at a clumsy government attempt to restrict the rights of the *parlements*, one of Grenoble's few distinctions being that it was precisely the seat of a *parlement*, thanks to its status as the capital of the Dauphiné. This event is generally identified by historians as an important precursor to the 1789 Revolution in Paris, not that Henry could have understood what was really happening, or the historical significance it would go on to acquire, but, then again, no other member of his family is likely to have done so either. Henry remembers seeing the blood of a protester who had been bayonetted in the small of his back and who died minutes later (*oi*, ii, p. 582), and also hearing an old woman scream, 'I'm revorting [*sic*]! I'm revorting!' (*oi*, ii, p. 583).

Around the same time, Henry allegedly met Mme d'Agoult-Montmaur, or, as Henry puts it, 'I met Mme de Merteuil' (*oi*, ii, p. 593), for she was the woman alleged to have served as Pierre Choderlos de Laclos' model for the Marquise de Merteuil in *Les Liaisons dangereuses* (Dangerous Liaisons, 1782), Laclos having been stationed as an officer in Grenoble; eventually, again allegedly, Stendhal was to meet Laclos in a box at La Scala while himself stationed in Milan in 1800–1801. Brulard tells us Mme de Merteuil fed him candied walnuts.[1]

Henry seems to turn up with unaccountable frequency a passive witness to Grenoble's infrequent brushes with political and literary history. It is fitting that he should have received a small act of kindness from Merteuil, for Henry's own revolt was very similar to hers: like Merteuil, he arrived at a set of principles in the self-reliant pursuit of freedom and thought of himself as his own creation. Indeed, one of Stendhal's most remarkable personal achievements was to recognize the Merteuils who crossed his path and genuinely to admire them. It is, after all, rare to find men who applaud women for their ruthless pursuit of freedom. He would go on to create a series of his own Merteuils, including the wonderfully self-reliant Mathilde de La Mole, who quotes Corneille's Medea on behalf of both herself and Stendhal: 'In the midst of so many perils, I still have MYSELF!' (*orc*, i, p. 645).

After his mother's death, and once the Revolution had hit its stride, executing Louis XVI and otherwise resorting to the Terror in a paranoid – or not so paranoid – bid to stave off the forces of reaction, an only slightly older Henry developed what Brulard describes as his 'instinctive, filial love' for the Republic (*oi*, ii, p. 552), as well as an ever deeper suspicion of the reactionaries who made up his birth family. In particular, he rejected any notion of filial duty to his actual father, 'the Bastard', announcing one day that if Chérubin loved him so much, then he could give Henry enough money to live his life as he pleased, for example by joining the Republican army as soon as he had come of age (*OI*, II, p. 624). It turned out that Chérubin did not love him so much – Henry compares his father's furious reaction to that of Tsar Nicholas I berating his inexplicably recalcitrant Polish subjects for insufficiently loving of his august person, dispassionately concluding that 'all tyrannies are alike' (*OI*, II, p. 624). It is at this time that Henry developed his passion for tyrannicides, quite literally so in the case of Charlotte Corday:

> All forms of tyranny revolted me and I did not like established power. I *did my exercises* (essays, translations, verses on the subject of a fly drowning in a bowl of milk) on a pretty little walnut table [. . .] I had the idea of writing on the wood of this table the names of all the assassins of princes, for example: Poltrot, the Duc de Guise, at . . . in 15 . . . My grandfather, as he was helping me compose my verses, or rather composing them himself, saw this list: his soul, gentle, tranquil, opposed to all violence, was saddened by it; he almost became convinced, as a result, that Séraphie was right to represent my character as atrocious. Perhaps I was prompted to compile my list of assassins by the actions of Charlotte Corday – on 11 or 12 July 1793, for I was mad about her. (*OI*, II, p. 726)

It did not matter to him what kind of tyrant these assassins killed, so long as they expressed their revolt through violence: that the killer, in Charlotte's case, should be a woman excited him beyond all measure, which perhaps explains the folly of his enthusiasm for her, no matter that the tyrant she killed was a Jacobin. Henry, of course, normally approved of Jacobins, but

Corday, a Girondin like Mme Roland, could not have appeared more attractive to him, hence, no doubt, his fantasy of himself as her widower. The glamour of Revolutionary violence never abated; nor did the appeal of brave, headstrong women unafraid of death – Mathilde de La Mole is at her most attractive when (spoiler alert) she takes possession of Julien Sorel's severed head. Similarly, Henry Brulard tells us he thrilled to Louis xvi's decapitation and never subsequently disapproved of it: 'I was seized by one of the most profound feelings of joy I have experienced in the course of my life. The reader may think me cruel, but I'm the same person at the age of 52 as I was at the age of ten.' (*oi*, ii, p. 634)

He continues:

I conclude from this memory, so fresh before my eyes, that in 1793, 42 years ago, I went about the hunt for happiness exactly as I do today; or, to put it more simply, my character was exactly the same then as it is now. All compromise when it comes to the interests of the *nation* still strikes me as *puerile*.

I would say *criminal*, were it not for my limitless contempt for those lacking in character. (For example M. Félix Faure [. . .] talking to his son [. . .] in the summer of 1828 about the death of Louis xvi: 'he was put to death by bad men'). (*oi*, ii, p. 635)

To Stendhal, the regicides remained forever tyrannicides, that is, heroes fighting for the survival of the Republic, their political violence fully justified. As an adult, he would go on likewise to justify the execution of a number of other more minor historical figures whom he regarded as traitors to the nation, whatever the horror his opinions inspired among his acquaintances: 'I can honestly say that I am utterly indifferent to the good opinion of people I consider to be *lacking in character*. They strike me as mad; I can see quite clearly that they do not understand what's at stake.' (*oi*, p. 635)

But how plausible is it that young Henry should have arrived at such unshakeably draconian republican idealism by the age of ten, or five, or four, or three? Only insofar as Henry's hatred of tyrants stood in for his hatred of his father. 'The Bastard' is not some random insult: as has already been noted, it reflects Stendhal's insight that all 'legitimate', that is, patriarchal, power is in fact illegitimate and that, if we are born slaves, whether to a father or to a king, it lies within our power to free ourselves from our unwanted masters, so long as we first learn, like Merteuil, to recognize that all claims to power over us are in fact fraudulent. (Of course, admiring illegitimacy as he did, Stendhal might also be according some small measure of grudging respect to his father by referring to him as 'the Bastard'.)

Henry's sense of himself as a revolutionary rested, to a large extent, on his perception of himself as a 'slave'. This perception, in turn, rested on his sense of his own isolation. The young Henry was kept away from other children, especially *common children* (*OI*, II, p. 608). This did little either for his mood or for his social development. In the *Vie de Henry Brulard*, Stendhal writes that he spent his moral life 'carefully considering five or six main ideas' (*OI*, II, p. 547). One of these, as we have already seen, was his attitude to political violence and, in particular, the Terror. Another, unquestionably, was his social engagement with people from a lower social class. Looking back as an adult, Henry notes that his political opinions have always been republican and that he has always admired the people of France: the citizens who came together to form the Republic. At the same time, he concedes that his parents successfully inculcated aristocratic tastes in him: cleanliness and good manners mattered to Henry, which is why, when he finally managed to attend a meeting of Grenoble's Jacobins, aged eleven, or possibly twelve, he found himself repelled by the unexpected absence of such genteel qualities:

I found them horribly vulgar despite wanting to love them [. . .]
In short, I was then exactly as I am now: I love the common people
and hate their oppressors, but it would be a never-ending ordeal
for me to have to live among them. (*oi*, ii, p. 686).

Put another way,

I have to admit that, despite being, at heart, perfectly
a republican in those days, my parents had just as perfectly
communicated their reserved and aristocratic habits to me.
This defect has stayed with me [. . .] I abhor having anything
to do with the rabble even though, when they are called *the
people*, I am passionately committed to their happiness [. . .]

I have a horror of everything dirty and the people always
appear dirty to me. The people of Rome serve as an exception,
but in their case their dirtiness is hidden by their ferocity.
(*oi*, ii, pp. 678–9)

He is not proud of these sentiments: it is just the way things turned
out. Forced to choose, in his life and in his fictions, he always opted
– I think and hope – for courage, warmth and generosity over wit,
polite conversation and manners. At least, I love him as a writer
in good part because, over and over again, he appears to make
that choice. Certainly, the precise nature of (his own) courage
and generosity can be added to the list of five or six main ideas
that Stendhal spent his life considering.

Another way of looking at all this is that Stendhal thought
obsessively about his profound loneliness and therefore about the
complicity and companionship that he craved. Julien Sorel's mother
never appears in *Le Rouge et le Noir*; as a result, he too grows up
isolated within his family – in fact, even more so than Henry – but
the psychological effect appears much the same. Insofar as there is
a key to Julien's character, this is it. He cannot believe that anyone

sincerely likes him, not even the youngest of Mme de Rênal's children, of whom he is particularly fond. Thus the thought that 'he at least does not yet hold me in contempt' is quickly replaced by the thought that 'the children stroke me the way they stroke the young hunting dog they bought yesterday' (*OI*, I, p. 403). If the narrator is to be believed, Julien is characterized as much by his 'complete absence of fellow-feeling' as by his 'hypocrisy' (*OI*, I, p. 415), hence his astonishing failures of generosity when it comes to Mme de Rênal, ironically the character who most believes in his generosity (*OI*, I, p. 383), for she is herself generous and so attributes her own qualities to him: 'in others, we can only esteem ourselves' (*HPI*, p. 235).

Stendhal likewise found it very difficult to believe that anyone sincerely liked him. It is for this reason that friendship appears in his texts, if anything, as an even higher value than romantic love, for romantic love is founded not just on reciprocal esteem, but far more problematically, on desire. Friendship, by contrast, rests solely on a reciprocal esteem that finds its expression in the sacred language that Stendhal spent his life trying to formulate. But it is precisely because Stendhal found it very difficult to believe that anyone sincerely liked him that all his life he sought out those who appeared to do so. Henry's childhood, marked as it was by his revolt against his family, his isolation and his inflexible republicanism, came in fact to be defined by his friendships with two grown men: Vincent Lamberton and Louis-Gabriel Gros. It is worth taking the time to try to understand why.

Stendhal's writings repeatedly return to the idea that human beings generally divide into con artists (*fripons*) and their marks (*dupes*): in any given interaction, one party becomes dominant and imposes its will on the other, generally to obtain some sort of benefit, usually, but not always, pecuniary. As Baudelaire, always a fine judge, was to observe of Stendhal: 'he was much afraid of being duped.'[2] François Leuwen, Lucien's father, eventually notes that 'the main way of being duped is to fall in love' (*ORC*, II, p. 457).

But, as we shall see, Stendhal was already well ahead of that particular game: as early as 1805, he had noted that 'the worst way of being duped takes the form of never falling in love, once one has come to know women, for fear of being played false' (*OI*, I, p. 213).

The status of the dupe or the con artist's mark is another of the five or six ideas that came to dominate Stendhal's moral life. The ideal to which Stendhal aspired was a state of grace or exception to the con artist/mark paradigm, which we might reframe as the narcissist/empath paradigm: what Stendhal was always hoping to find, at whatever personal cost, was a perfect exchange of empathetic goodwill, founded on open communication and allowing for unresolved disagreement. On this last point, Mérimée reports that Stendhal would shut down discussions with his friends once an obvious difference of opinion had emerged with the words 'You're a cat, I'm a rat' (*HB*, p. 445). The sacred language of friendship is not to be employed to persuade others to see the world the way one sees it oneself; if anything, it serves to bring out the differences that friendship alone can accommodate.

Stendhal's fictions include numerous representations of perfect friendships. These are often between members of the same sex: in *Le Rouge et le Noir* and *Lucien Leuwen*, respectively, Fouqué is to Julien and Gros is to Lucien what Mme Derville is to Louise de Rênal and Mme de Constance is to Bathilde de Chasteller. Occasionally, even more exceptionally, they cross and blur the gender divide: Théodelinde de Serpierre and Lucien are friends in this sense, esteeming each other and conversing freely, despite the marked differences of their outlooks. All these fictional friendships find their origins in their author's childhood.

The first of Henry's own intense friendships was not with a boy or girl of his own age, but with Vincent Lamberton, Dr Gagnon's valet, known to him as Lambert. Insofar as the young Henry managed not to feel isolated after the death of his mother, it was thanks to Lambert, but when Henry was ten, Lambert died, three days after falling from the branches of a tree. Writing in his fifties, Henry observes,

> Where today is the memory of Lambert still to be found, other than in the heart of his friend?
>   I'll add this, who still remembers Alexandrine [of whom more later], who died in January 1815, twenty years ago?
>   Who still remembers Métilde [of whom much more later], who died in 1825?
>   Are they not mine now, do they not belong to me who loves them more than anyone else in the world, who thinks passionately about them ten times a week and often for two hours at a time? (*OI*, II, p. 679)

Stendhal knew that, in life, the answer to his rhetorical question was in fact no, these people did not belong to him, for people do not belong to each other, or they would not be free. However, in death, maybe things are different? There's an interesting slippage in the passage just cited between his love for his friend (Lambert) and for two women to whom he made sexual advances that were comprehensively and in the latter case indignantly rebuffed. What Brulard is expressing here is the grief of his loss: all three individuals, differently, but finally equally, made Henry feel that he was not alone when he found himself admitted to their sweet proximity, and to that extent, he loved them all in exactly the same way, for all three possessed his esteem, which is another way of saying that all three allowed him to esteem himself in them.

Skipping forward to 1830 and his Parisian middle age, Stendhal ruefully observes that there is not a single one of his current friends who would not be delighted to see him drenched in filthy water were he to step out onto the street in fine clothes. Silly though this example may seem, to Stendhal such innocently petty spite was enough to damp the ardour of his own sentiments. In his fiction,

Stendhal also explores such pettiness between friends, for example in his account of the relationship between Lucien Leuwen and Coffe. Lucien's tactless, blundering goodwill meets with Coffe's laconic, fair-minded, but finally cold and detached judgementalism. Stendhal's fictional friendships mostly do not suffer from such defects. His fictional love affairs are much messier, founded as they are not just on esteem, but on desire.

The critic René Girard has identified Stendhal as perhaps the most important of a series of authors – also including Flaubert, Dostoevsky and Proust – to have anticipated his own anthropological theory of mimetic desire. Stendhal, so Girard argues, came to understand that we think we desire directly, but actually can only ever desire what we believe others to desire. The primary relationship is therefore not with the nominal object of one's affections but with the mediator of that object: the rival. The pattern set up is once again antagonistic: a battle between an eventual winner and an eventual loser for a doubtful illusory prize. Stendhal both had that thought and found it unbearable, just as he found unbearable the thought that all friendship might in fact be no more than disguised competition. To this extent, and almost only to this extent, Stendhal was a Romantic. He believed in the possibility of true friendship, entirely exempt from rivalry, and even in the possibility of true love, entirely exempt from external mediation, for he appears to have believed that desire could, however fleetingly and infrequently in a nineteenth century largely devoid of heroism, take the form of sincere, reciprocated passion, founded not on rivalry, but rather on mutual esteem and the mutual exercise of what he terms 'the faculty of wanting' (*vf*, p. 37).

Clearly, Stendhal's wanting to believe in the reality of friendship and love would not have been enough to prevent these concepts from turning out to be illusory and, having spent his life trying to develop the critical distance that would allow him to see things as they are, the horror of discovering that his isolation was in fact radical and incurable would not have been enough to prevent him from acknowledging that true examples of friendship and passion can only be found in fictions such as the novels he would one day write. However, when Brulard was twelve, the course of his intellectual and moral life was again decisively altered, this time by a series of experiences that convinced him he was not, after all, radically alone.

3

Truth, 1795–9

Brulard's slavery to his birth family had been made inexpressibly worse by what Henry portentously refers to as the 'Raillane tyranny' (*OI*, II, p. 604), for in his bid to prevent Henry from playing with common children, Chérubin entrusted him to the care of tutors. The first of these, a certain Joubert, wasn't up to much before helpfully dying. His dreary replacement was Jean-François Raillane, a Jesuit in the fullest sense, seen by Henry as a filthy and morally and physically repulsive hypocrite. The aim of the education Raillane provided was to reinforce the aristocratic values of Brulard's family – its misguided sense of its own dignity – and to pervert the idealism of his young charge. It also tended to treat truth as both in and of itself suspect and an irrelevance:

> One day, my grandfather said to the Abbé Raillane:
> 'But Sir, why teach the child Ptolemy's system of astronomy when you know it to be false?'
>   'Sir, it explains everything and is in any case approved by the Church.' (*OI*, II, p. 611)

Dr Gagnon, a man of science and the Enlightenment, was shocked, but did nothing to intervene. There could surely only be one outcome to Raillane's sustained campaign against truth: Henry would eventually succumb to the parental and societal pressure being exerted on him, cease being atrocious and instead become

Anonymous artist, *Jean-François Raillane*, 18th century, engraving.

a crook (*coquin*), like so many others before and since – in the process, he would stop being his own singular creation, stop being a Merteuil.

Had Raillane succeeded in his alleged endeavour, there would be no biography for me to write: Henri Beyle would have gone on to try to accumulate wealth and secure his social position in Grenoble, no doubt using his father's connections to become a lawyer of some sort. He would have met family and class expectations: become another Candide Chenevaz. But Henry resisted, in part thanks to the influence of his great-aunt Élisabeth. The value she placed on personal honour and greatness of character meant she had very little time for stuffed shirts, including even her sweet-natured and cultivated brother. Throughout his own life, Stendhal wondered if he himself possessed greatness of character, whether in his thoughts or in his deeds: did he exemplify the qualities of generosity, courage, enthusiasm and authenticity embodied by his exemplars, Élisabeth included? Certainly, he wished to be singular. Why limit oneself to the words and behaviour expected by others, ideally to be reproduced only ever ironically and antiphrastically when in the presence of stuffed shirts, if one can instead speak and act impulsively, unpredictably and authentically when in the presence of friends? This, in essence, is *beylisme*: a defence and assertion of the singular self.

Élisabeth's influence, however, also left Henry vulnerable, for it prevented him from seeing things as they are. It led him to overestimate the iniquity of others, starting with his unfortunate father Chérubin, aunt Séraphie and sister Zénaïde. It also led him to overestimate the worth of others, starting with his sister Pauline. Finally, it led him to adopt Élisabeth's habitual hauteur, which worked against both his own and her instinctive generosity. The discovery of mathematics and logic – the discovery of truth – would, therefore, prove a welcome antidote not just to the values promoted by Raillane, but to those embodied by Élisabeth. It would allow him to think dispassionately of things as they are, starting with himself and his family.

As has already been noted, Stendhal would eventually come to see that his father had been devastated by Henriette's death and that his father's coldness was probably first a manifestation of extreme grief and then a response to that son's own evident hostility; possibly it even led him to the realization that his father would have been perfectly entitled to pursue any sexual interest he might have had in Séraphie. Stendhal also came to see himself for what he was: a stocky, unattractive boy, anxious and odd, destined to grow up to be a stocky and unattractive man, at times very much in control of himself and at others not at all, perduringly anxious and odd despite all his increasingly confident displays of wit and intelligence.

The Raillane tyranny came to an end in 1794 when the ghastly Jesuit unexpectedly disappeared to take up a better job elsewhere. Then, in 1795, the Republic, Henry's ideal parent, opened a school in Grenoble: Dr Henri Gagnon was called upon to lend his prestige to the foundation of this École Centrale. Perhaps as a result, and much to his delight, the twelve-year-old Henry was allowed to attend. Immediately, he felt part of a wider community of boys, or rather, he felt part of the Republic. His teachers were mostly of at least some inspiration and gave him a reasonable grounding in a range of disciplines. His favourite subject was, without doubt, mathematics, deemed the pure manifestation of truth: 'How ardently did I adore the truth at that time! How sincerely did I consider it the queen of the world I was about to enter!' (*OI*, II, p. 858) But M. Chabert, his mathematics teacher, found it difficult to answer Henry's questions. Unable to explain and resolve the contradiction between two separate accounts of the properties of parallel lines, Chabert left Henry doubting whether his teacher was after all an adept of 'the cult of truth' (*OI*, II, p. 858). Was Chabert finally any different from Raillane? It is at this point, Stendhal claims, that he reached the first of two crossroads. Discouraged, he appears to have come quite close to submitting, that is to say suppressing his own critical *LO—GIQUE* and so becoming a hypocrite. Had he done so, Henry optimistically argues, he would have become a rich man. But at what price?

This moment made a huge impression on him. He felt on the brink of giving up something he valued intensely about himself: the independence of mind – or 'spirit of examination'– that went with isolation. Now ensconced in the École Centrale, what could be easier than to conform, swapping the singularity of his opinions and beliefs for easy and superficial companionship, and even for advancement?

Anonymous pseudo-portrait of Stendhal in his library, 19th century, oil painting.

I almost gave in. An able confessor, a proper Jesuit, would have been able to convert me at that moment by expatiating on the following maxim:

'You can see that all is error, or rather that there is no such thing as either truth or falsehood, everything being a matter of convention. Adopt the convention that will most help you to be received by polite society. The rabble is Republican and will always sully that cause; side with the aristocracy, like the rest of your family, and we'll find a way of sending you to Paris and of recommending you to women of influence.' (*oi*, ii, p. 859)

He could so easily have become a crook (*fripon*) at this point: succumbed to the vast Jesuit conspiracy begun by Raillane, and turned into a con artist – the drama of this Faustian struggle is replayed at some length in *Lucien Leuwen*. But fortuitously a second crossroads was reached, and the risk of giving in was definitively averted. In the process, Brulard and Stendhal both learnt, emotionally rather than intellectually, that friendship and love are indeed the products not of rivalry but rather of esteem.

Henry had been agitating to be given private lessons in mathematics, having identified a plausible tutor in Louis-Gabriel Gros, a surveyor and notorious Jacobin – his surname would eventually be given to Lucien Leuwen's closest male friend. Eighty-year-old great-aunt Élisabeth 'generously' (*oi*, ii, p. 860) came up with the necessary cash. Her heart and intelligence were those of a thirty-year-old, Henry observes (*oi*, ii, p. 860): she had made it to 28 a long, long time ago and had barely aged since. Henry arranged for his first lessons.

What Brulard has to say about his first encounter with Gros, at the age of twelve, may appear hyperbolic, even absurd. Yet I would argue that he here gives his fullest attention to trying to express the exact truth of the matter:

In the end, chance had it that I saw a great man and did not become a crook. Here [. . .] *the subject exceeds what can be expressed in words* [the phrase is borrowed from Charles de Brosses: 'le sujet surpasse le disant']. I shall try not to exaggerate [. . .]

Encountering a man on the model of the ancient Greeks and Romans immediately made me want to die rather than not be just like him. (*OI*, II, pp. 859–61)

Gros was the first of what Brulard refers to as his 'passions d'admiration' (passionate admirations):

I adored and respected him so much that perhaps I displeased him. I have so often encountered this surprising and disagreeable reaction that it is perhaps as a result of an error of memory that I attribute it to the first of my passionate admirations. I displeased M. de Tracy and Mme Pasta by admiring them with too much enthusiasm. (*OI*, II, p. 863)

In *De l'Amour*, Stendhal defines love as admiration plus hope, which we might re-express as the formula: love = esteem + desire. Stendhal's experience of friendship, at least after this first meeting with Gros, produced the even simpler formula: friendship = esteem. It is for this reason that Stendhal sometimes signed off his letters to close friends 'salutation and esteem'. The absence of desire, as between Henry and Louis-Gabriel – not that Louis-Gabriel was not a beautiful man, all estimable people being beautiful: Stendhal believed that our habits of mind come to be etched on our faces – did not prevent esteem alone from manifesting itself as a form of passion. In all cases, whether autobiographical or fictional – as in the case of the friendship between Lucien Leuwen and Théodelinde de Serpierre – the intensity of this relation is founded on an esteem that takes the form of a profound and justified sense of the other's exemplarity. Henry did not just like Gros, he wanted to be just like Gros.

All of Stendhal's fiction would eventually turn on this notion of exemplarity. Mostly, Stendhal's exemplars are historical or fictional – that is, in both cases, made up. But Stendhal had actually met some of his exemplars: not just Gros, Destutt de Tracy and Giuditta Pasta, but also Napoleon and La Fayette. We do not compete with our exemplars: we model ourselves on them, which is very different. They are in no way our rivals. We do not desire them, but rather esteem them, sometimes passionately.

Gros' exemplarity took two different forms. He was, very clearly, Henry's teacher, somebody who could finally be trusted to understand more and to explain what he understood. In other words, Gros possessed a superior perspective and was willing to let Henry share in it, to see through his eyes. But there was more to it than that: as has already been noted, Gros was a Jacobin, enthused by the new political ideals of the Republic. He had very little social standing but, despite his poverty, appeared in no way servile. He had a pride about him, as demonstrated particularly by the care he took over his appearance. Gros was in no way filthy or repulsive, whether physically or morally – he was the anti-Raillane, providing an example of freedom that helped his young charge overcome the last effects of the Raillane tyranny.

Stendhal is a writer much given to decrying vanity, which he identifies as having been a driving force within French society at least since the Renaissance, but which he believes became pervasively dominant only after 1815. What Stendhal means by vanity is caring about the perceptions of others and pretending to be what one is not in order to obtain social advancement – being a stuffed shirt. To a very large extent, Stendhal's concept of vanity overlaps with what we might today term narcissism. But what he does not mean by vanity is pride. Mathilde de La Mole is a case in point: generations of critics have fallen over themselves to identify her as vain, narcissistic and therefore wrong-headed by Stendhalian standards, despite her being so manifestly right-headed by these same standards in so many of her ideas. Yet Mathilde's awareness of what others think of her is very carefully distinguished by Stendhal, and by his narrator, from the impulse to pander to the expectations of others that marks almost everyone else in her society – including, to a very large extent, Julien. Like Gros, Mathilde is proud: she wishes only to satisfy herself and to live up to her own personal standards. From Stendhal's perspective, we ought to esteem Mathilde: want to be like her, just as Henry wanted to be like Gros.

For Henry, Gros' Jacobinism was finally neither here nor there. Mathilde admires Mme Roland and Danton in the same way that she admires Queen Marguerite de Navarre: esteem is not ideological, that is, constrained by what Stendhal dismisses as 'partisanship' (*ORC*, I, p. 614). In *Lucien Leuwen*, the fictional Gros is, in fact, made less admirable by his Republicanism, his vapid political utopianism clearly preventing him from seeing things as they are and making him at times dull company. Stendhal was, in fact, a political atheist, or put another way, a moderate liberal who thought most political opinions stupid. Writing as M. Van Eube de Molkirk, a characteristically silly pseudonym, Stendhal notes that he will be denounced as 'a Jacobin, a Bonapartist, a sans-culotte, a lackey of Empire, etc.' (*s*, p. 57) – Stendhal was very fond of the dismissive 'etc.' that allowed him to dispense with tiresome detail, his friends having already understood him perfectly well. Van Eube de Molkirk goes on: 'The truth is that if I did have any political opinions to express, they would belong to the *centre left*, like those of the vast majority of people, and that I was born too late to have played any active role in the Revolution.' (*s*, p. 57).

But the French Republic was more important to Stendhal than all this might suggest: all his life, Stendhal also remained committed to the affective charge of loyalty – and paranoia – engendered in him by the French Republic at the time of the Terror. Stendhal was a sensible liberal who nevertheless believed in political violence as the only way for the individual to fight against protracted injustice. As we shall see, Stendhal is the only major author of the French nineteenth century actively to have considered trying to assassinate the head of state.

The Republic was founded when Stendhal was nine; it was in effect, although not formally, suppressed when he was sixteen. The formative years of his childhood therefore played themselves out against the backdrop provided by a series of sensational political events. At the time of the Terror in 1793, Chérubin Beyle became politically suspect and briefly had reason to fear for his safety – he successfully hid in Dr Gagnon's spare bedroom, which puts the zeal and competence of his persecutors into their proper perspective. Monstrously, young Henry's sympathies were with the Republic.

On the national stage, Henry came to admire many of the leading revolutionaries, starting with Mirabeau and Grenoble's own Barnave before settling very clearly on Mme Roland and Danton as his hero(in)es. The former was, by the time she was executed, a moderate. The latter played a part in her downfall as a leading member of the radical grouping known as *La Montagne*, before himself quickly succumbing to the Terror. Stendhal wanted to be both of these exemplars, just as Mathilde de La Mole wanted to be Mme Roland and Julien Sorel wanted to be Napoleon. As we have already seen, Stendhal valued the Revolution for the opportunities it gave to individuals to reinvent themselves by inhabiting new, freer identities; in a still more limited sense, he appears to have valued it for making him personally happy, not just by persecuting his father – lovely though that was – but thanks to the exemplary spectacle it provided.

As Stendhal surveyed the Revolutionary era, particularly with hindsight, he came to identify the familiar antagonism between con artists and their marks. The Girondins, Mme Roland included, were marks: idealists, eager to imagine that ordinary men and women would spontaneously rise up not just to defend the Republic but to participate freely, actively and disinterestedly in its functioning. Girondins, Stendhal decided, were no good at issuing orders to other people – as we have already noted, one of the definitions of happiness as far as Stendhal was concerned was to issue no orders and to obey none himself. Danton, by comparison, was a con artist, not unlike Napoleon. Both stole money and were otherwise corrupt;

Anonymous artist, *Chérubin Beyle*, 19th century, oil painting.

both abased themselves by employing expedients in the squalid pursuit of power. Nonetheless, Stendhal identifies Danton's organization of the Republic's defence by a conscript army and Napoleon's Italian campaigns as the two grandest events in modern history, made possible precisely by Danton's and Napoleon's ability to issue orders and to have them obeyed.

Mérimée tells us that Stendhal was never of the same opinion twice when it came to Napoleon. The historian Pieter Geyl takes this negative assessment and runs with it: according to Geyl, Stendhal never stopped to think about the emperor's career – never troubled his head about the purpose of the 'energy' he attributed to his hero.[1] It is easy to see how Geyl could have arrived at this conclusion, and easy also to see how the generosity of Stendhal's outlook might have confused not just Geyl, but even Mérimée, astute though the latter could sometimes be about his friend. But, in reality, Stendhal spent an enormous amount of his time troubling his head about Napoleon's career.

Brulard looks back at his adolescent self and notes with no little shame that Napoleon's glamorous rise had been enough to turn his young head: 'I accuse myself of having had this sincere desire: that the young Bonaparte, whom I imagined to be a handsome young man like a colonel in an *opéra comique*, should make himself the King of France.' (*OI*, II, p. 864) Henry had failed to see Napoleon for all that he was – failed to see the truth. For Napoleon, if anything even more than Danton, was not just a leader of men, but a con artist. The charisma that seduced Henry from afar, as he followed the young general's exploits first in Italy and then in Egypt, would eventually seduce him in person: Napoleon and later La Fayette were the two political figures who made the biggest personal impression on him, no doubt in part because both were also soldiers who had exhibited personal courage and generals who had demonstrated that they could win a battle – neither was a hypocrite in these two senses at least. But if Stendhal's admiration for Napoleon as a great man on the Greek or Roman model – a modern-day Alexander or Caesar – never faded, his political assessment, especially of the emperor that Napoleon became, was to prove highly nuanced, and not only in retrospect.

4

Empire, 1799–1815

Henry's school career ended with a series of prizes, including the prize for mathematics, although he was less the prodigy of his imagination than an enthusiast. Nevertheless, by the age of sixteen it had become clear that he would be a plausible candidate for the elite École Polytechnique in Paris. With the unqualified support of his family – now minus Séraphie who had died in 1797, which perhaps explains the unqualified support – Henry shipped himself off to Paris with a view to preparing for the entrance exam. He arrived in November 1799, exactly one day after Napoleon's coup d'état of 18 Brumaire. Napoleon was indeed about to become the King of France, or rather, in relatively quick succession, First Consul (1799), First Consul for Life (1802) and Emperor (1804).

Henry found Paris, the capital of his beloved Republic, much less glamorous than expected. In particular, he was shocked by the lack of mountains and the prissily pollarded trees. Stendhal liked both trees and humans to be allowed to grow wild. As has already been noted, Stendhal had never thought much of Grenoble. He had been quite pleased by its early role in the Revolution and by the fact that it briefly was known as 'Grelibre', as a play on the way it had turned against the nobility by championing the cause of liberty. He took for granted its natural setting, at the confluence of two valleys, surrounded by imposing mountains, until he realized that not all cities were similarly blessed. But mostly, he thought ill of his hometown, referring to it contemptuously by its Gaulish name,

Cularo, presumably with the stress on the *cul* (arse). By contrast, he came to think of Paris, the city in which he died and is buried, as the only truly tolerable place in France in which to live. What he valued about the capital was its status as a republic unto itself, whatever the nominal system of government currently holding sway over France as a whole. In particular, he would eventually discover that it was possible to live anonymously in Paris, in a fifth-floor apartment, 'solitary and mad as a Spaniard, a million miles away from real life' (*OI*, II, p. 538). The very reasons Rousseau found to dislike Paris and view it as a vast Babylon led Stendhal to think of it as the last bastion of freedom. For the time being, though, Henry Brulard found himself unexpectedly homesick in Paris.

Very quickly, Henry started to formulate a new plan of (in)action, possibly with a view to frustrating yet further his family's expectations. Stendhal never did take the exam for the École Polytechnique, contenting himself with eventually sending Octave de Malivert and Lucien Leuwen, two of his fictional characters most closely modelled on Henri Beyle, to that *élite* institution. Instead, after a period of illness and apathy, and again with the support of his family, eager to see him make a career or rather finally earn an income for himself, Stendhal hitched his wagon to his Parisian cousins, the Darus.

Noël Daru, the patriarch, and his son Pierre were quite good cousins to have in the age of Napoleon. Noël was well connected, rich and crafty, so Pierre was already making a brilliant career for himself as a bureaucrat, one that would eventually see him rise to the most senior civilian position within Napoleon's imperial war machine. This would, of course, prove useful, but nowhere near as useful as it ought to have been.

Stendhal never mastered the art of schmoozing Pierre Daru – his eventually falling in love with Alexandrine Daru, Pierre's wife, cannot have helped much either, although she appears to have found a way of averting complete disaster on Stendhal's behalf. Nor did he

Copy by Virginie Géo-Rémy after Antoine-Jean Gros (1771–1835), *Pierre Daru*, 1813, oil painting.

ever master the art of impressing his notoriously hard-to-please patron – he got off to a bad start, mistranscribing the relatively simple word *cela* as *cella* when taking dictation (*oi*, II, p. 920), before going backwards. Henri Beyle could come across as a complete idiot, not least when he wasn't concentrating, but even when he was. Pierre Daru, 'that volcano of insults' (*oc*, II, p. 920), had made a profession out of not suffering complete idiots gladly or indeed at all. Looking back, Henry Brulard thinks he knows why: Pierre Daru was 'furious and always angry about something because he was himself *always afraid*': 'he lived in mortal fear of Napoleon and I lived in mortal fear of him' (*oc*, ii, p. 919).

To start with, the Darus made do with welcoming their anxious and odd provincial relative, helping him recover from his illness. Pierre then had him appointed to a supernumerary position in the Ministry of War. Stendhal was a mixed bag as a bureaucrat. When he focused, as during Napoleon's retreat from Russia, he appears to have been capable of getting through an enormous amount of work quickly and well. When bored, he appears to have done very little work, slowly and badly – notoriously, he would go on, as a consul in later life, to send a coded message in the same envelope as its cipher, possibly as a joke or a show of contempt, but equally possibly as a mark of his continuing capacity for complete idiocy. What he started to learn in 1800, and then continued to learn after 1807, was how to write reports by bringing together different sources. It was a method that he would go on to apply to his non-fiction writing: the art of *précis*, or, as it is sometimes otherwise called, plagiarism.

Stendhal soon tired of being shouted at as an unskilled clerk in a pretend job. He decided to cash in his chips with Pierre Daru in exchange for an army commission. Short on training, experience and aptitude, Henri Beyle was made a second lieutenant in the dragoons. Finally he was realizing his ambition to leave his family and join a Republican army, for France was still nominally a Republic, despite Napoleon's coup. Stendhal's first posting took him to the scene of the First Consul's great triumphs at the head of the Republican army: Italy.

Stendhal has a tendency to tell the story of his life, whether in autobiography or in fiction, in such a way as to bring the reader with him as far as the first discovery of Italy and then to break off the narrative, there being no words to describe certain subjects. In general, Stendhal finds it difficult to talk to us about his feelings at moments of supreme emotion because to do so would be to cheapen those experiences, the way that Romantic literature cheapens what it is to feel something, especially when that Romantic literature is written by Chateaubriand. Stendhal would go on to settle for a deliberately dry writing style. He famously wrote, in the draft of a letter to Balzac of 1840, that, when composing *La Chartreuse de Parme*, he would read a few pages of the Napoleonic Code to find the right tone. 'Allow me to express myself crudely: I don't want to wank off [*branler*] the reader's soul' (*CG*, VI, p. 411).

The more emotional Stendhal becomes, the more laconically, or crudely, he expresses himself: the final page of *La Chartreuse de Parme* is an object lesson in emotional continence precisely because the emotion of the characters is, at this stage in the narrative, entirely incontinent in its intensity. But sometimes it is not enough even to be emotionally continent: only an abrupt lapse into silence will do. There is an irony, here: Stendhal gives his name to the modern-day Stendhal syndrome, an affliction imputed by Italians to the tourists who flock to Rome, Florence and Venice and find themselves overcome by the beauty of the cityscapes on show. To experience the shock of first encountering Italy in Stendhal's manner has come to mean to gush inanely, even though, to recap, Stendhal in fact found it very hard to write about his first experience of Italy. We know of his arrival, over the Mont Cenis pass (he loved the Alpine scenery), and of his descent through the Valle d'Aosta: familiar, partly Francophone territory, not dissimilar culturally or geographically from the French part of Savoy that neighboured the Dauphiné. We then know of his arrival in the Lombard plain and his entry into Milan.

Something of the euphoria of this first experience of the city can be found in the opening chapter of *La Chartreuse de Parme*, recounting the triumphant entry into Milan of Napoleon's Republican conscript army in 1796. Henry arrived in 1800, the other side of the Treaty of Campo Formio of 1797. He dates Napoleon's fall from grace surprisingly early: not to 1815 after Waterloo, nor to 1814, when he was first comprehensively defeated, nor to 1813, when he was retreating chaotically from Moscow, nor to 1804, when he had himself proclaimed Emperor and formally brought the Republic to an end, nor even to 1799, when he staged his Caesarist coup, but to 1797, when, despite all his rhetoric in support of Italian freedom, he occupied and then pragmatically ceded Venice and the Veneto to the Austrians. 'Here ends Napoleon's heroic phase' (*N*, p. 618):

> The occupation of Venice in May 1797 marks the end of the poetic and perfectly noble part of Napoleon's life. Thenceforth, in order to safeguard his position, he had to resign himself to measures and expedients which were no doubt perfectly legitimate, but which can no longer give rise to passionate enthusiasm. (*N*, p. 571)

Put yet another way still, 'In 1797, one could love him passionately and unreservedly; he had yet to rob his country of its liberty; nobody of his grandeur had emerged for centuries' (*N*, p. 253).

For all Napoleon's moral decline, the Milanese court of his stepson and viceroy, Prince Eugène de Beauharnais, is repeatedly cited as a byword for glamour in *La Chartreuse de Parme*. Certainly Stendhal, as a young second lieutenant, found Milan and its environs a congenial place. Privileged young men had, of course, been finding all of Italy a congenial place for generations. Stendhal, used only to the drab provincialism of Grenoble and the Republican asceticism of Paris, suddenly found his life transformed: over a very short period of time, he had his first ice cream, tasted his first proper coffee, went to his first opera, lost his virginity, contracted syphilis and fell in love with Angela Pietragrua, who would eventually become his mistress on his return to Milan in 1811. Add to that allegedly sitting next to the author of *Les Liaisons dangereuses* in a box at La Scala, and you have a pretty overwhelming set of experiences for any seventeen year old.

Stendhal appears not to have had all that much to do as a soldier: he probably spent a lot of 1800–1801 thinking about sex. It used to be argued by literary critics that Stendhal's novels were written as exercises in wish-fulfilment. All of Stendhal's heroes are young and physically attractive in a way that gives rise to considerable sexual interest from his young and physically attractive heroines. The sex that is not described between these characters is simply fantastic – the sex that is described much less so, for it becomes worth describing precisely as it begins to subside into risible imperfection. It is hard to imagine Stendhal having perfect sex with anyone, even as a young man, not least given his own foregrounded accounts of intermittent erectile dysfunction, but actually his journal records what sounds like a lot of high-functioning sex with a very wide variety of women. Stendhal came especially to admire a number of these sexual partners, most notably Angela Pietragrua and Albers de Rubempré, but equally lots of other women with whom he did not have sexual relations. There are many times in his writings, whether fictional or private, when he quite clearly posits women as falling into two categories: potentially agreeable sexual partners and potentially agreeable conversational partners. He and his characters think of seducing the former but come to adore only the latter. Thus Stendhal describes Henry Brulard in Vienna in 1809 as 'having a mistress I was screwing [*que j'enfilais*] and a mistress I adored' (*OI*, II, p. 916). Lucien Leuwen likewise ponders the merits of having 'a mistress in two volumes': 'Mme de Chasteller for the pleasures of the heart and Mme d'Hocquincourt for less metaphysical moments' (*ORC*, II, p. 333). But actually Stendhal appears more aware than any other male French author of the nineteenth century I have come across that the purpose of women is not to divert men, but rather to satisfy themselves: his final novel, *Lamiel*, is seemingly written with the specific object of making this point as forcefully as possible. Stendhal's various pronouncements quite often take the form of bravado, often calculated to chime with, and mock, the known prejudices of his interlocutors. This bravado also proceeded from his shyness, for let us not forget that Stendhal was, in his private thoughts, chiefly anxious and odd. In particular, Stendhal was often timid around the people he loved, remaining loyal to them long after they had broken off all contact, just as he remained loyal to the memory of Lambert.

In his young adulthood in Italy, Stendhal was particularly shy and self-conscious, especially around women. He endeavoured to conquer his timidity by learning how to have sex using exactly the same method he employed to learn how to do everything else: by studying the theory of the act, at least insofar as his sexually predatory fellow soldiers purported to understand it, in the hope of discovering in advance exactly what to do and say at the moment of performance (*oi*, i, pp. 20–21). Mérimée reports that, until the age of thirty, Stendhal had it as his rule, or at least so he claimed, to try to seduce any woman with whom he found himself alone: '"It pays off one time in every ten attempts", he would say. "Well, the chance of one success in ten makes it worthwhile to meet with nine rebuffs"' (*hb*, p. 455). Mérimée goes on to say that Stendhal 'had suffered, as so many others do, from shyness in his youth. It's a difficult thing for a young man to enter a salon. He imagines everyone is looking at him and is always afraid of not behaving *correctly*' (*hb*, p. 455). Stendhal therefore devised a method for appearing calm in such situations, which consisted of making no changes to his bearing until such time as 'the emotions of entering had passed' (*hb*, p. 455).

Stendhal both dreaded and enjoyed performance. In particular, he made it his business to use performance to overcome his physical and mental disadvantages: his portliness, his timidity, his anxiety, his oddity. Surely, then, we can assume that he used his fictional alter egos, whether male or female, simply to erase all of his imperfections, or rather to substitute them with perfections: for portly, anxious and odd, read svelte, brave and singular.

However, this would be to miss the further point that the physical beauty of his fictional hero(in)es is intended as a joke on the profane reader, in thrall to conventional ideas of what we ought to envy in others, for their sexual attractiveness in fact works against them every bit as much as it works for them. Stendhal's hero(in)es find themselves again and again reduced to their physical beauty, as though their intellect and their courage pale by comparison. To be physically beautiful, Stendhal concluded, is to remain, in some senses, invisible, precisely on account of the attention one attracts, just as passing for plain produces a different invisibility, on account of the attention one fails to attract – in *Les Liaisons dangereuses*, Merteuil writes approvingly about the value of invisibility and in particular about the time for observation and reflection that invisibility creates for the unfairly overlooked. For his part, Stendhal observes in *De l'Amour* that on the second day of acquaintance, beautiful people appear more ordinary, for the initial shock of their physical appearance has by then passed and this diminution of interest further obscures their real qualities (*DA*, p. 95); plain people, on the other hand, may generate sudden interest by revealing qualities of intelligence or character on the second day. As Stendhal argues, explicitly and implicitly, what we hold most dear in the people we love are their imperfections, of body and of mind, perhaps because these imperfections function as the signifiers of the intellect and courage and singularity that constitutes their real beauty. All that said, Stendhal gives every impression of knowing what it feels like to know oneself to be physically ugly and to observe not just intelligently, but invisibly and enviously, those generally understood to be beautiful. In this sense, the awkwardly tall (as opposed to fat) and physically ugly Théodelinde de Serpierre in *Lucien Leuwen* functions as Stendhal's double, conceiving as she does a tender friendship for Lucien that 'wasn't love, for the poor girl didn't dare; she was well aware of, and perhaps even exaggerated to herself, the defects of her height and her face' (*ORC*, II, p. 386).

The young Stendhal sought to make up for his natural disadvantages by playing to his acquired advantages: his imagination and his logic. Another way of putting this is that he sought, with what we have already seen Gide refer to as 'inverted sincerity', to imagine himself as the person he wanted to be and then actually to become this person through a long process of habituation. Yet another way of putting this is that he sought not to delude himself but rather to see himself as he was, also as a means of understanding how others saw him. His chief object, nevertheless, was to make himself estimable, in his own eyes and, possibly even more importantly, in the eyes of those he himself esteemed. This process started in childhood. It would take him a long time to realize that even those who appeared to disdain him in fact also in part esteemed him, just as those who esteemed him also in part disdained him; it took him even longer to come to terms with that thought, for Stendhal trained himself to perceive other people in as much layered detail as possible, but would then be hampered by an impulse to accord them either all or none of his regard. He wanted either to adore as he adored his mother or to detest as he detested his father, to extend his esteem as he extended this to Pauline or to evince his contempt as he evinced this to Zénaïde – it is possible he came to understand that he never really knew anything solid about any of those people and that both his esteem and his contempt were frequently misplaced, although not always so.

After a while, towards the end of 1801, Stendhal tired of his life in Italy and decided to return to Paris to dedicate himself more fully to study and, for the first time, to literature. If Milan had proved the equivalent of a gap year, the bulk of the next five years was given over to serious study, with the exception, towards the end of that period, of a brief adventure in Marseille.

Stendhal's real motive for returning to Paris may well have been his desire to become a famous writer or, put more accurately, to acquire literary glory. Whether military or literary, glory always appealed strongly to him, perhaps because glory alone justifies pride. But, as Lucien Leuwen puts it, 'How can one talk about true virtue, glory or beauty to fools who understand nothing and try to sully with their mockery everything that is delicate?' (*ORC*, II, p. 636). To Stendhal, glory was real in a way that literary reputation was not. He was fond of observing that the journalist Simon Linguet was as famous in his own era as Voltaire, more so even. Salvandy was similarly a famous and respected writer in Stendhal's era. But Stendhal would come to understand that his own best works were lottery tickets that would one day win him literary glory, however posthumous; the tickets of Linguet, Salvandy and the other stuffed shirts who come to dominate any given literary market would, instead, be certain never to come up.

Armed with such insights, Stendhal set about acquiring his first ticket. He decided to write an epic poem, to be entitled *La Pharsale* (The Pharsalia). Stendhal may have been thinking of the way Voltaire greatly contributed to his early glory by producing an epic poem, *La Henriade* (The Henriad, 1728). Eventually, Stendhal was to acquire the insight that the novel would become the dominant genre of the nineteenth century, but in 1802, the epic poem seemed both more prestigious and timeless.

Already on 9 March 1800 Stendhal's first extant letter, written to his sister Pauline, had advised her to read Plutarch's Greek *Lives*, as these had 'formed the character of the man with the most beautiful soul and greatest genius ever, Jean-Jacques Rousseau' (*CG*, I, p. 4). By 22 January 1803, much preparatory reading and theoretical study having been undertaken in order to create the right conditions for *La Pharsale* to emerge, Stendhal wrote to his sister Pauline with the discovery that Plutarch was in fact more important even than Rousseau: his *Parallel Lives*, it turned out, constituted 'the book of books: whoever reads it properly discovers that all other books are but their copies' (*CG*, I, p. 71). Plutarch was the mother lode: almost all recent political events could be traced back to the *Lives* of his Greek and Roman heroes. Henry's insight when he met Gros turned out to have a more universal application: Mme Roland, and Danton and Napoleon, were all Plutarchan heroes for the modern age, men and women of the Greek and Roman model, and to recognize them as such was to want to die if one couldn't be just like them. What better material for stirring literature? Maybe *La Pharsale* would allow Stendhal to produce an artful allegory of recent political events? Bound to come up as a winning combination.

The year 1802 also saw the publication of Chateaubriand's *René*, the dominant urtext of what would become the French version of Romanticism, eventually parodied by Stendhal in *Armance*. Chateaubriand could see that the epic poem would not, in fact, turn out to be the genre of the age. His antihero, René, was characterized by extremes of inaction and self-pity, all rendered in sonorous prose. Stendhal was repelled, at the time and throughout his life: 'in general, I have to say, once and for all, that Chateaubriand's ways of thinking, the gloominess of René, etc., could not be more opposed to [my] own way of thinking' (*OI*, I, p. 1075). Chateaubriand was mediocre and false, a hypocrite and a liar, all posturing and fake emotion, forever '*branl*[*ant*]' his readers (*CG*, VI, p. 411). Moreover, literature had to be about men and women who did things, however foolishly, with the aim not just of wasting their lives away. They might be tyrannical, they might be idealistic, but literary hero(in)es should never be inactive. Rather, they should turn themselves into modern-day versions of Charlotte Corday or Napoleon, Marcus Brutus or Julius Caesar. Stendhal was beginning to see that from Plutarch had sprung Montaigne and Rousseau, as well as a new wave of European tragedians, most notably Schiller and Vittorio Alfieri. To that list, he hoped eventually to add himself.

For the time being, Stendhal was focusing on a very specific type of Plutarchan hero: the great generals and conquerors, for example Julius Caesar, as his bombastic choice of subject demonstrated. The Battle of Pharsalus saw Caesar gain a decisive victory over Pompey's republican forces in the civil war. As one biographer, Victor Del Litto, points out in some perplexity, 'it seems curious that, at a time when young Beyle claims to adhere to the most intransigent Jacobinism, he should admire the figure of Julius Caesar.'[1] As he goes about composing his poem, Stendhal defines Caesar in overtly Napoleonic terms. Some thirty years later, Stendhal would still be writing of Napoleon as 'the greatest man to appear in the world since Caesar' (*N*, p. 257).

So did Stendhal indeed hopelessly detach himself from his childhood Republicanism and embark on a career as a craven apologist for Napoleon's evident will to power? Henry Brulard comments that in this period he had wished for two things: to study the political and military career of Turenne, a leader of men and conqueror admired by Napoleon, and 'to write comedies like Molière and live with an actress' (*OI*, II, p. 537). So much for the idealism of youth. But in 1803 Stendhal's interest in *La Pharsale* started to wane and he instead conceived of a new project, *Les Deux Hommes* (The Two Men), about a con artist and his mark. In a marginal note Stendhal compares the dupe, an idealistic product of an Enlightenment education, to Caesar's assassin, Marcus Brutus. By July 1804, a couple of months after the Senate had proclaimed Napoleon Emperor, Stendhal was clear in his mind that Brutus was the Plutarchan exemplar he most admired. Napoleon was out, intransigent Jacobinism was back in. From this point on, whatever his personal enthusiasm for the emperor, Stendhal appears consistently aware that the empire itself was a more or less enlightened tyranny. For example, 'from 1807 onwards, I passionately desired that he [Napoleon] fail to conquer England, for where would one then find asylum?' (*OI*, II, p. 858).

As Stendhal went about pursuing his literary endeavours, he was also busy acquiring a general education. His approach was methodical, based around a self-devised programme of study. His aim was to turn himself into a philosopher, a product not just of the Enlightenment, but of more contemporary thought, most notably as produced by Ideologues such as Destutt de Tracy and Cabanis. Dutifully, Stendhal ploughed through textbooks and treatises. It was just like going to university. But it wasn't helping him to write great literature, or indeed any literature. In July 1805 he ran away to Marseille to live with an actress. By the middle of 1806, he was back in Paris, where he appears to have noticed that Pierre Daru was significantly further advanced in his stellar career. It was time to stop reading and to give up on the idea of writing: it was time instead to *do* something.

In many ways, this was the lesson that Stendhal spent the two years from 1804 to 1806 trying to teach himself. In particular, Stendhal had come to understand that he had fallen too much under the spell not so much of Plutarch but of Rousseau – Rousseau and Napoleon would eventually become the two dominant influences on Julien Sorel in *Le Rouge et le Noir* and likewise conspire to drive him a bit mad. If Stendhal's life in Paris did indeed see him become 'solitary and mad as a Spaniard' (*OI*, II, p. 538), it was in large part because of his tendency to judge events using his imagination – in *Le Rouge et le Noir*, we are eventually told that this is 'the error of a superior man' (*ORC*, I, p. 672). If he came to 'venerate' Cabanis, Destutt de Tracy and Jean-Baptiste Say (*OI*, II, p. 538), it was in a bid to rid himself of this error, although even his engagement with hard-headed logic took the form of unbridled enthusiasm.

On and off, Rousseau had been a dominant influence on Stendhal since his teenage years. As early as July 1804, however, Stendhal was starting to see that this influence might have been unhealthy:

Construct my soul in such a way as to allow it the greatest possible happiness in the career that I expect to follow. I'll be

happier and frequently less virtuous [. . .] For example, last year
I was made unhappy by my hatred for tyrants; I've been happier
this year now that I hate them less. Yesterday, I read the life of the
divine Brutus (Marcus, not Junius). It restored my hatred for
tyrants, and since yesterday I've again been unhappy [. . .]

Hatred for tyrants has been my strongest passion after my
love of glory.[2]

There are a number of things to be said about this note to self. First,
it confirms Stendhal's determination to do something with his life.
Octave de Malivert and Lucien Leuwen, the two male characters
most closely based on Stendhal's own affective life, and even the
impulsively energetic Julien Sorel, all run the risk of failing to develop
their potential, giving way instead to the ever more concentrated,
ever madder thoughts that swirl restlessly in their minds. Stendhal
always gives the impression of constant, restless thought. He had a
cult of energy; he was easily bored; he had a need to express himself,
often using too many words. In adult life, he was self-assured and
strong-willed, vivid and extrovert, overwhelming and overpowering,
prone at every turn to challenge social norms and the injustice they
seek to legitimate. He had a cult of generosity and cared little for
money. He was extraordinarily sensitive, to himself and to others,
and still really quite odd. He appears to have spent the bulk of his
life trying to make that oddity work for him and staving off the
recurring temptation to kill himself. If Stendhal valued singularity,
it was no doubt because he was himself singular.

His experience of the Revolution and his studies, not just of the
Ideologues, but of the philosopher Maine de Biran, from whom he
derived his key idea of habituation – that is, the active training of
perception as opposed to the passive experience of sensation – all
predisposed him to the project of self-construction. At the very
heart of this project, again and again, we find Rousseau just as we
find Plutarch and Stendhal's other key idea of emulation. All his

adult life, Stendhal sought to habituate himself to respond according to the character he wished for himself, in emulation of the historical figures he most esteemed: Caesar, Danton and Napoleon; Marcus Brutus, Charlotte Corday and Mme Roland. But he also understood that emulation could lead to the madness of quixotry and the paranoid delusions of Rousseau.

Rousseau's sense of himself as relatively good and natural in the midst of corrupt civilization prompted him to use *Les Confessions* to construct a narrative of himself to which he endeavoured to conform in his life. There was a problem though, as Stendhal increasingly came to acknowledge: Rousseau couldn't see things as they were, having fallen peculiarly prey to his imagination. In particular, Stendhal appears acutely sensitive to Rousseau's paranoia, no doubt because he was himself, to some extent, paranoid. As Mérimée puts it,

> People claim that the police were everywhere under the Empire, and that Fouché knew everything that was being said in the salons of Paris. Beyle was convinced that this gigantic network of spies had retained all its occult power. As a result, he surrounded his every minor action with all manner of precautions. He would never write a letter without signing it using an assumed name: César Bombet, Cotonet, etc [. . .] and often he would start it with a sentence such as 'I have today received your raw silk which I have sent to a warehouse pending its shipment.' (*HB*, p. 456)

In part, these were reasonable precautions for someone whose adulthood was spent dodging the intrusions first of Fouché's secret police and then of the Austrian police in Milan – he would eventually be thrown out of Milan in 1821, having come under suspicion of working as a spy, quite possibly because he never signed letters in his own name. But Stendhal was also simply paranoid, which is no doubt why Baudelaire intuited that he had a great fear of being made a dupe. Such paranoia came to define his emotional life as well. In one of the complements to *De l'Amour*, he defines love as a function of paranoia – 'To be in love is always to be fearful' (*DA*, p. 343) – and, as we've already seen, his entire system of friendship was founded on the notion that he feared only those he esteemed. But was Stendhal more than merely anxious and odd: was he in fact 'mad as a Spaniard' (*OI*, II, p. 538)?

When we consider his obsessive desire to be esteemed and to esteem, his paranoia and his documented tendency to contemplate suicide, we might conclude that he suffered from what might today be termed a borderline personality disorder. I think it much more likely that he was extremely perceptive and self-mocking, had read a lot of Rousseau and had made a conscious moral choice to be sincere and generous in his dealings with others. Stendhal – possibly like Octave in *Armance* – was not so much mentally ill as a Romantic.

Stendhal valued sincerity because he wished to make himself known to his friends. Similarly, he hoped to make sense of his friends by dint of generosity. This last concept rested on Stendhal's empathetic attempt to see the world from the perspective of others, possibly also in order to find out the worst of what others thought of him – hence the paranoia. It is never good to find out the worst of what one's friends think of you, particularly if you come across as singular. If Stendhal's friends thought the worst of him, probably this was because they found it hard to make sense of his singular and suspicious nature. Put another way, they were probably quite frightened by his powers of perception as suddenly revealed to them in moments of inexplicable insight. They appear not to have really understood how he thought. It is thanks to this understanding that he could use his novels to reveal, in quite astonishing detail, the processes by which his protagonists think. It is the detail of his understanding of how minds work – what he more generally terms 'the genius of suspicion' (*OI*, II, p. 430) – that makes Stendhal a 'question mark of a man' and 'France's last great psychologist', to quote Nietzsche (himself, of course, quite singular).[3] In particular,

Stendhal used self-analysis and the analysis of his friends and exemplars in order the better to construct himself.

There appear to have been two impulses behind Stendhal's decision to construct himself: the desire to make himself estimable, if not to the general run of his peers then at least to himself and eventually to the happy few; and the desire not to give himself up entirely to paranoia, misanthropy and apathetic isolation. It was time to invent a relatively stable imaginary self to which to conform.

This imaginary self would have a career, playing its part in society. The decision to participate actively in a corrupt world is analysed at length in *Lucien Leuwen*: it comes down to Montaigne's advice to 'grapple with necessity' (*ORC*, II, p. 369). How can one know anything about oneself if one refuses to engage with the world and to assert oneself, as well as the counter-normative values one holds dear? As Stendhal put it to Mérimée when the latter announced he was starting to learn Greek, aged 25, 'You're on the field of battle [. . .]; now's not the time to polish your rifle; you need to start shooting' (*HB*, p. 455).

Stendhal's imaginary self would come to be defined by the related philosophies contained within his notions of *beylisme* (a term that first surfaces in Stendhal's writings in 1811) and *égotisme* (which Stendhal associates particularly with his return to Paris in 1821). For the time being, though, it was largely defined by a rejection of Rousseau's influence (and the equally brooding influence of the Italian tragedian Vittorio Alfieri) in favour of what he would go on to term the hunt for happiness.

Stendhal coins the verb *dérousseauiser* in a journal entry of 21 November 1804. It was then that he committed himself fully to the study of Destutt de Tracy, Cabanis and a broad range of other contemporary thinkers. The aim was to 'de-Rousseauize my judgement' (*OI*, I, p. 152), that is, temper his Rousseauvian proto-Romanticism with realism, by which he meant a logical, detached – and if at all possible, amused – apprehension of things as they are.

At heart, this was a Voltairean project. Of the major novelists of the nineteenth century, Stendhal's birth in 1783 made him by far the most eighteenth century of the major novelists of the nineteenth century. The title of *Le Rouge et le Noir* is, in addition to the many other things already discussed, a nod in the direction of Voltaire's *Le Blanc et le Noir* (The White and the Black, 1764): Stendhal's novel plays endlessly and artfully with a range of eighteenth-century intertexts, functioning at times especially as a three-way dialogue between Stendhal, Voltaire and Rousseau.

On 30 April 1805, Stendhal lays a bout of 'madness' at Rousseau's door; on 6 February 1806, he says he should resolve himself to become a hypocrite; and so on. The need to shrug off Rousseau's influence, and with it the dupery of sincerity, appears as a thread running through Stendhal's writings all the way up to 1811. A first attempt to grapple with necessity led him, in July 1805, to run off to Marseille to live with the actress Mélanie Guilbert. Given Rousseau's stated horror of the theatre, this was a promising start. While in Marseille, Stendhal additionally decided to try his hand at commerce by working for an export company, Charles Meunier & Cie. Quite rapidly, the world of business ceased to appeal, and so, against all the odds, did living with an actress.

Stendhal was easily bored. He could be very charming, especially with women, whom he tended very much to like, as well as with children, whom he finally could not be bothered with, but whom he refused to patronize with hypocritical nonsense – a refreshing change for them, then as now. It is one thing to charm, though, and quite another to cohabit. Stendhal found domestic life extremely difficult, even in its highly approximate and unconventional form as Mélanie Guilbert's live-in lover.

Mérimée observes wearily that 'I never once saw him not in love with a woman or thinking himself so' (*HB*, p. 449). Brulard, for his part, tells us that 'For me, love has always been the most important thing in my life, or rather the only important thing' (*OI*, II, p. 767).

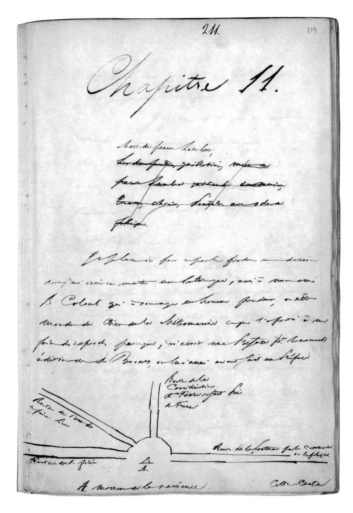

Page from the *Vie de Henry Brulard*, written and drawn in Stendhal's hand, setting out the paths his life could have taken: the path of madness; the path of the art of making oneself read; the path of worldy success; the path of acquiring wealth through commerce or position. The starting point A is the moment of birth (*oi*, ii, pp. 670–71).

What Stendhal meant by love is artfully picked over in *De l'Amour* and then in the first four of his novels. The fifth, *Lamiel*, is very radically written from the perspective of a highly intelligent young woman, and so finds nothing but amused contempt for the love that men have to offer. Stendhal truly did understand that love takes the form of a will to power: 'true passions are selfish' (*ORC*, I, p. 469); 'all true passion thinks only of itself' (*ORC*, I, p. 559). He also understood that passion was no more than euphoric infatuation, which, in his case, on account of his sincerity and his powers of empathy, he could sustain indefinitely, albeit mostly intermittently so. Mérimée offers the following testament to the constancy of Stendhal's infatuations:

> He'd just seen Madame Curial, then aged 47, and had found himself to be every bit as much in love with her as on the first day. They'd both had many other passions in the meantime. 'How can you still love me at my age?', she'd said. He'd shown her how very well, and I never saw him betray so much emotion. He was welling up as he told me about it. (*HB*, pp. 449–50)

The states and phases of Stendhal's infatuations are described in amused, self-critical detail in *De l'Amour*, and then again in the novels. In *Le Rouge et le Noir*, Julien Sorel famously falls in love with two women: Louise de Rênal and Mathilde de La Mole. In a complement to *De l'Amour*, Stendhal observes that 'Nobody can give themselves over to two loves' and 'A new love chases out the old' (*DA*, pp. 341–3). These maxims are illustrated by the third, generally less remarked upon love of Julien's life: Amanda Binet. Amanda works behind a bar in Besançon; Julien enters the bar; he falls in love with her; he quarrels with a man whom he perceives as his rival for Amanda's affections; they come close to fighting; he leaves; Amanda is forgotten. But perhaps, if he had ever seen her again, he would immediately have reverted to loving her.

rêve de nuit

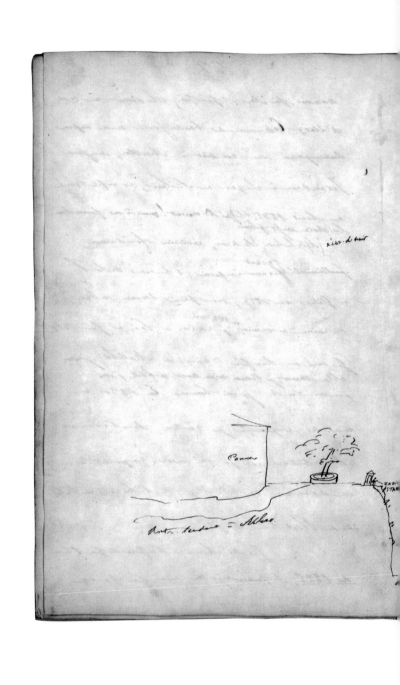

Commune

Route tendant à Athos.

A page spread from the *Vie de Henry Brulard*, written in Stendhal's hand, listing the loves of Stendhal's life (*OI*, II, p. 541).

Biographies of Stendhal always run the risk of losing themselves in Stendhal's love affairs, whether consummated or not. At any given moment in time, he is in some phase or other of courtship. In 1802, he fell in love with a cousin, Adèle Rebuffel; not long after, he was sleeping with her mother; in 1803, he fell in love with Victorine Mounier; not long after, he was in Marseille cohabiting with Mélanie Guilbert, having met her while taking lessons with the actor Dugazon. Napoleon famously took acting lessons from François-Joseph Talma. In part, Stendhal was following the emperor's example; in part, he was trying to prepare himself for a career as a playwright.

Given that Stendhal is about to head off around Europe in the wake of Napoleon's armies, with a view to having as much sex as possible, I do not propose to chronicle his romantic life *in extenso*. Instead, I shall follow Brulard's prudent lead and focus only on those relationships that reshaped Stendhal's outlook and therefore helped define both his sense of self and his fictions. Chivalrously, Brulard lists twelve such relationships, but there are essentially only six: Wilhelmine (more usually given as Mina or Minette) von (more usually given as de) Griesheim, Angela Pietragrua, Métilde Dembowski, Clémentine Curial, Alberthe de Rubempré and Giulia Rinieri. Other women mattered to him enormously also, whether he wanted to sleep with them or not, but insofar as his relationships allowed him to rethink everything about the way human beings engage with each other, these six were the ones that mattered.

Stendhal left Mélanie Guilbert to her career, abandoned his own and returned to Paris in the summer of 1806. On 3 August of that year, he joined a masonic lodge. But Stendhal also had the Darus to fall back on, and they were suddenly proving themselves to be incredibly useful. Less than three months later, Stendhal accompanied Martial Daru, Pierre's much-less-daunting brother, to Berlin, arriving in Napoleon's wake on 27 October. A few days

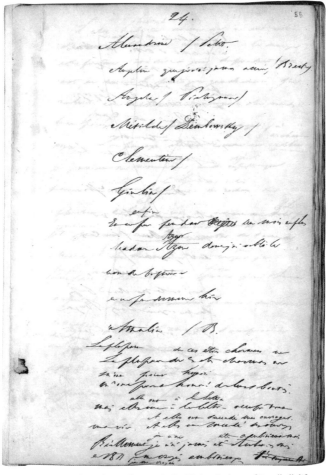

Second of two pages from the *Vie de Henry Brulard* listing the loves of Stendhal's life (*OI*, II, pp. 541–2).

later, Pierre Daru appointed him to a provisional position as an imperial administrator in Brunswick. On 13 November, he arrived to take up his first proper post. He was suddenly launched in his career as a bureaucrat.

It was while he was in Brunswick, trying to learn how to be a civilian and military administrator, how to write administrative reports and how to get on with the understandably frosty local notables, that he met Mina de Griesheim, a model for the heroines of *Mina de Vanghel* (composed 1829–30), *Tamira Wanghen* (composed 1837) and *Le Rose et le vert* (The Pink and the Green, composed 1837), as well as, more obscurely, for Bathilde de Chasteller in *Lucien Leuwen*. What is immediately striking about the narrative of *Mina de Vanghel* in particular is how self-willed its heroine appears: there is no sense of her wishing in any way to fit around, or meet the expectations of, the male object of her affections. Rather it is he who is expected to meet her expectations, such as they are, for actually, even when she is thinking about him, she is in fact thinking only of herself. Mina de Griesheim was haughty, distant and self-absorbed, while also being capable of sincerity. What is striking about the majority of the women Stendhal pursued is that sense of fierce independence, bordering on a complete lack of cooperation.

The reason Stendhal has frequently been identified as a proto-feminist is that he consistently places his female characters at the centre of their own narratives, seemingly valuing women precisely for their agency as subjects, including as sexual subjects. Stendhal consistently identifies women as being freer than their oppressors, more sexually dominant than their male lovers, more intelligent than their male peers, braver than the men who imagine themselves heroes, less conventional than even the most singular of their suitors. He also consistently identifies them as possessing the hauteur of a Mme Roland, a Charlotte Corday or a Mina de Griesheim, whatever their outward appearance of either boldness or timidity. All women, Stendhal seems to think, potentially possess such hauteur, for they have met men and been left unimpressed.

Stendhal tells us he never did manage to sleep with Mina who, undeniably, possessed hauteur. In *De l'Amour*, he revealingly tells us that there isn't a man alive who wouldn't swap half of his remaining

Stendhal as bureaucrat, here in a portrait attributed to Edme Quenedey (1756–1830), *c.* 1807, physionotrace charcoal portrait.

days for the chance to see the woman he loves naked. Female nudity, including that of his mother when he was an infant, was important to Stendhal: more so, it would seem, than sex – in *De l'Amour*, he suggests that sex is only really satisfying if timed correctly at the peak of obsessive interest. Sex for Stendhal was finally more a physical than a cerebral pleasure, and therefore both coarse and secondary. Stendhal expressed his love for women by talking with them.

Anonymous artist, *Minette (Mina) de Griesheim*, *c.* 1820, miniature portrait.

Admiration, esteem, or the recognition of what Stendhal refers to as merit, each play a huge part in Stendhal's definitions of love. Certainly, he admired Mina de Griesheim. Certainly, also, he could never have settled down with her, particularly not in Brunswick, nor anywhere. He records her squeezing his hand on one occasion, and that appears to have been enough for him. What he really wanted to do was to one day write about her. As for his immediate sexual needs, he appears to have found it quite easy to meet these, first in Brunswick and then on a series of further bureaucratic missions, every new assignment bringing with it a new set of potential assignations.

Stendhal's gradually accelerating administrative career took him from Brunswick, where he had been permanently appointed as an adjunct War Commissar on 11 July 1807, to a more glamorous post jointly administering the newly created Department of the Ocker in Westphalia. He was authorized to style himself an Intendant of the Imperial Domains and, for the first time in his life, found himself a person of some consequence, at least in his own little corner of Napoleon's empire.

Perversely, he decided to mark his elevation with a return to thoughts of writing. Part of 1808 was given over to an ill-starred history of the War of the Spanish Succession: even with such a gift of a topic, he was still struggling to find his voice. More positively, he managed to find a way of leaving Westphalia, first for Paris, then for Vienna – where, in 1809, he attended a performance of Mozart's *Requiem* to mark the death of Haydn a few days earlier – and thence to Hungary. Busy as he was, he found the time to fall in love with Alexandrine Daru, the wife of his patron Pierre. What part attempted career suicide played in this unexpected turn of events is hard to gauge. She appears to have been very fond of him, which is, no doubt, why he fell in love with her, and to have been really quite extraordinarily patient in her dealings with him.

It is at this point that he visited Salzburg and saw the salt mine that would lead to his famous theory of *cristallisation*: the process of falling in love is likened by Stendhal, in *De l'Amour*, to taking a stick and throwing it into a salt mine. When you pull the stick out, it is covered in crystals and so looks much better than it really is. Love is not about things (or individuals) as they are, but rather things (or individuals) as we reimagine them. Love is quixotic. There's a limit, I think, to how interesting or helpful this image actually is, but it has ended up as something for which Stendhal is quite widely known.

In 1810, he again returned to Paris, and it is at this point that he became somebody not just in his own eyes, but in the eyes of his peers. In August, he was appointed as an auditor in Napoleon's Conseil d'État, finally joining the fast stream. Stendhal celebrated by falling in love with an opera singer, Angéline Bereyter, considering marriage to a certain Jenny Leschenault and then choosing this precise moment to declare himself to Alexandrine Daru – who very kindly rebuffed him with a minimum of fuss on her part – before heading off on a tour of the west of France in the company of two childhood friends, Louis Crozet and Félix Faure. He then took another period of leave and returned to Milan in 1811, where his new wealth and status appears to have prompted Angela Pietragrua to see him in a radically new light. He declared himself, a mere eleven years after first falling for her, and they quickly became lovers. He then set off on a triumphal tour of Italy, all in some style. Life would never be this good again, at least looked at from a vulgar perspective.

Stendhal's long Italian idyll eventually came to an end and he returned to Paris, where Napoleon was preparing his next campaign. Stendhal would be allowed to join the Grande Armée in its assault on Russia. The march on Moscow and subsequent disastrous retreat are the only major historical events from the Napoleonic period that Stendhal witnessed at first hand – he was in Vienna at the right time for the battle of Aspern-Essling, but wisely stuck to sightseeing; he was ill and stayed in bed for the battle of Wagram, despite his claim in the opening paragraph of the *Vie de Henry Brulard* to having witnessed it. Understandably, neither battle made a particularly strong impression on him, except perhaps in his imagination.

Stendhal arrived in Moscow on 14 September 1812, working on his new literary project, of which more later, and contracting a fever. While there, he rescued – or looted – a book from one of the burning houses: Voltaire's *Facéties*. Mérimée tells us that Stendhal felt a kind of guilt on account of its being a volume from a magnificently bound set of Voltaire's works, now rendered incomplete thanks to him. On 16 October, Stendhal headed off back west to Smolensk, arriving only on 2 November. It was not an easy journey at that time of year, made yet more difficult by Cossack harrying. His mission was to organize supplies for the retreat. This he managed to do, receiving Pierre Daru's congratulations in the name of the emperor for

Jacques-Louis David (1748–1825), *Alexandrine Daru*, 1810, oil painting.

eventually providing the Grande Armée with bread somewhere between the town of Orsha and the Bobr River on or around 23 November – these would be the only rations they would receive as they made their way back to the natural obstacle provided by another river, the Berezina.

Stendhal was very interested in the question of whether or not he was brave. At various points between 1800 and 1812, he had

First page of a letter by Stendhal to his sister Pauline, 5 May 1810, at 2 o'clock in the morning: Stendhal is responding to the news that a former flame, Victorine Mounier, is getting married, by bemoaning his relative poverty and the consequent impossibility of his marrying (*CG*, II, pp. 24–5).

found himself confronted with real danger, and he was pleased, on the whole, with how he had comported himself at those moments. But Russia was to provide a quite different sort of challenge, to which, admittedly mainly by his own account, he rose magnificently.

We know from Mérimée the stories Stendhal subsequently told his friends of this period in his life. Many of these focus on the calm he was determined to keep in a crisis. This calm was the product of habituation, Stendhal having taught himself tricks to master his emotions at moments of great peril. Thus Mérimée tells us that when fighting a duel, Stendhal would preserve the appropriate sangfroid by looking at a tree while his opponent was taking aim and counting its leaves (*HB*, p. 455). He needed all his sangfroid now, for he was about to re-cross the Berezina and so participate in one of the most horrific episodes in European military history:

> One morning, in the vicinity of the Berezina, he appeared before M. D[aru], clean-shaven and dressed with some care. 'You've shaved!', M. D[aru] told him. 'You have a stout heart.' M. B[ergonié], one of the Auditors of the Conseil d'État, told me that he owed his life to B[eyle]. Foreseeing how congested the bridges would become, he had made him cross the Berezina the evening before the rout. It had almost been necessary to employ force to get him to walk a few hundred yards. M. B[ergonié] hailed the composure shown by B[eyle], as well as the good sense which did not fail him at a time when even the most resolute were losing their heads. (*HB*, p. 448)

To put Stendhal's self-possession and foresight in perspective, the following day around 80,000 men tried to cross a partially frozen, marshy river in sub-zero temperatures under continuous Russian bombardment. The bridges were soon destroyed, so four hundred Dutch engineers built a pontoon bridge out of scrapwood that required constant repair as it collapsed under fire. Four Swiss infantry regiments fought a rearguard action to protect the Dutch as they worked for hours in the water. Only eight of the Dutch engineers survived, and only three hundred of the 4,000 or so Swiss. Russian eyewitnesses reported the eerie spectacle of dead Dutch engineers suspended in the ice of the river, still clutching their tools.

Stendhal appears to have been fascinated by the overwhelming majority that collectively lost their heads, and by the minority that kept theirs, even as they lost their lives. He was likewise fascinated by later routs of the French army. Mérimée goes on to report the following alleged incident:

In 1813, B[eyle] by chance witnessed an entire brigade being routed by the unexpected charge of five Cossacks. B[eyle] saw approximately two thousand men, including five generals, identifiable by their brimmed hats, all in full flight. He was running away with the rest of them, with difficulty, for he was wearing one of his boots and carrying the other in his hand. Only two men out of the entire French corps proved brave enough to confront the Cossacks: a military policeman [. . .] and a conscript, who managed to kill the policeman's horse while trying to fire at the Cossacks. B[eyle] was given the task of reporting on this mass panic to the Emperor, who heard him out in a cold fury, whilst turning in his hands one of those iron contraptions designed to hold window shutters in place. An attempt was made to find the policeman in order to award him the Legion of Honour, but at first he tried to hide, before denying that he'd been present at the engagement, convinced that nothing good can come from attracting attention to oneself in a rout. He thought he would be shot. (*HB*, pp. 448–9)

On his return from Moscow, Stendhal was discouraged, exhausted and chronically ill. He had been hoping for a posting in Italy, there to resume the high life of 1811. Failing that, he had been hoping to be promoted to the rank of prefect and given his own department to administer. Instead, he was overlooked, possibly on account of his failure to hide his contempt and boredom when mixing with his peers, possibly because he was not in fact as good at his job as he liked to think he was.

In *Le Rouge et le Noir*, Stendhal uses two epigraphs attributed to Danton: the first, as has already been noted, points the reader to the truth, the bitter truth; the second reads, 'Oh Lord, grant me mediocrity!' (*ORC*, I, p. 749). We might envisage Stendhal's failure to advance further in his career in the light of these two epigraphs. The bitter truth is probably that Stendhal's chief qualities – his wit, powers of perception, decisiveness, irritation when presented either with details or with fools – made him a lot of enemies among the many people who had succeeded in advancing themselves precisely by never demonstrating any of these peculiarities; there is a further bitter truth that his singularity made him suitable only for a position of leadership and yet he was forever being asked to follow. The even more flattering way of saying all of this is that Stendhal was in no way mediocre – one has but to read a page by him to realize this basic fact about the man – and his superiority could not but help get right up the noses of his contemporaries. Stendhal's novels lightly represent the plight of singularity and superiority drowning in an ocean of mediocrity. But in his own life, there must have been a great deal of sadness at the indifference with which his best efforts were met. The last of the five or six main ideas that kept him occupied throughout his adult life was unquestionably the idea of failure.

In the spring of 1813, having spent a couple of months resting in Paris and catching up with both Mélanie Guilbert and Angéline Bereyter, Stendhal was packed off by Pierre Daru – very much against his will, his enthusiasm for the empire, as opposed to the emperor, having long been dissipating – to help organize the defensive campaign against Prussia. He left Paris on 19 April; passed through Dresden to have a look at some paintings by Correggio; observed the battle of Bautzen; and eventually witnessed the rout reported by Mérimée. As a result of this last incident, Stendhal was allegedly invited to a private interview with Napoleon, who again allegedly went so far as to touch him, grabbing his lapel in a moment of high emotion (*cg*, ii, p. 644) – it's just about possible that this really happened. Certainly, Stendhal submitted a report on the rout (*cg*, ii, pp. 416–17) and had 'a long conversation with His Majesty' (*cg*, ii, p. 419).

On paper, Stendhal's career peaked in June 1813, when he was named intendant of the province of Sagan (now Żagań) in Lower Silesia (now in Poland). He had become the equivalent, however temporarily, of a prefect, at the head of his own 'government', 'playing at being a tyrant' (*cg*, ii, p. 397). It was dull work. In July, he fell ill; in August Pierre Daru took pity on him and allowed him to return to Paris; in September he was back in Milan, for no good official reason, trying to make what sense he could of the mixed reception accorded to him by Angela Pietragrua; in November he set off back to Paris, via Grenoble, where Dr Gagnon had recently died; in December he was sent from Paris back to Grenoble, tasked with organizing the defence of the Dauphiné – things had not been going well for Napoleon. When would it all end? Soon enough.

5

Métilde: *De l'Amour*, 1815–21

In the *Vie de Henry Brulard,* Henry makes what he himself
acknowledges might appear to be a surprising statement about
his attitude to the fall of Napoleon: 'I fell in April 1814, at the same
time as Nap[oleon]. I came to Italy in order to live as I had done
in the Rue d'Angivillers [. . .] Who would believe it, but, as for me
personally, this fall gave me pleasure' (*OI,* II, p. 540).

Stendhal had had enough of empire. It was time to start again,
to return in spirit to the apartment where he had spent all of 1803
studying with a view to becoming a writer, and to return in body to
Milan, his elective hometown. It is there that Stendhal would come
the closest to falling in love and consequently learn to become a
writer, although when he first arrived, he thought he was already
in love and already a writer.

Stendhal had been working on and off on a variety of literary
and (art) historical projects as he stumbled his way along the
various connecting carriages of the imperial gravy train from 1807
to 1814. He produced nothing of any great interest in this period,
but, then again, his heart wasn't really in it. On 1 September 1810,
he used his last will and testament to stipulate the founding of an
annual literary prize to run in perpetuity, spreading his glory in
rotation to London, Paris, Berlin or Göttingen (for how to choose
between them?), Naples and Philadelphia (*OI,* II, pp. 989–91): he
was imagining the outsourcing of his literary career, no longer
having the time to bother with such trifles himself, not now that

he had prospects and fine clothes. Somebody else could do the writing and earn him the posthumous literary glory he craved. It is in this period of his life that he tried to become – and in the meantime to pass himself off as – a member of the new imperial aristocracy. In particular, he hoped to touch his father for enough money to buy himself the title of baron, and started signing himself Henri de Beyle. Brulard notes of this phase in his life, 'in reality, I've never been ambitious, but I thought I was in 1811' (*OI*, II, p. 542). Like so many of his generation, and ours, he had been seduced by wealth, status and the illusion of power. Put another way, he had become ensnared by the pleasures of social competition, or what Rousseau terms *amour-propre*, and so was gravely at risk of becoming the kind of stuffed shirt he had spent most of his life abhorring.

Stendhal appears to have recognized the possibility, and even the likelihood, that, as moderns, we are all, always and everywhere, engaged in social competition, often for pathetically low stakes; it would follow that we can only ever serve as rivals to each other, even when we find ourselves face-to-face with the people to whom we feel closest. It is for this reason that we can only ever be either con artists or their marks, one-up or one-down in a perpetual struggle for futile dominance. We can never feel respect or esteem or affection, only spite and the impulses to best and control the other – hence Stendhal's rueful account, already alluded to above, of the friend-ships, or should that be the diffident acquaintanceships, he enjoyed at the height of his bureaucratic career: 'When I go out into the street in a new, well-tailored suit of clothes, my friends would give five francs to see someone throw a glass of dirty water over me. I haven't put that very well but it expresses a truth.' (*OI*, II, p. 807)

Yet Stendhal's account of rivalry in friendship and, by extension, in love – it is in this period that he briefly cohabited with Angéline Bereyter, whom he dispiritingly claims in the *Vie de Henry Brulard* never to have loved (*OI*, II, p. 541) – is actually double. Rivalry, it turns out, can lead us not only to envy and the impulse to control, that is, to ill will and lovelessness, but to respect, esteem and generosity, that is, to goodwill and love. For rivalry encourages us to measure ourselves against others and therefore to admire those we believe exhibit some form of superiority; and it is from admiration that goodwill and love are both born.

Stendhal often experienced the positive emotions that proceeded from meeting someone who successfully incarnated one or more of the ideals towards which he himself wished to tend. It is in this sense that 'in others, we can only esteem ourselves' (*HPI*, p. 235): we admire in others the qualities we believe we ourselves possess, in however attenuated a form. And it is in this sense that Stendhal remained all his life ambitious: he longed to be able sincerely to admire himself, having judged himself dispassionately on his actual merits, in the same way that he admired others – Gros, Mme Roland, Charlotte Corday, Napoleon, Giuditta Pasta, Destutt de Tracy. For example, Stendhal esteemed Napoleon for the way he too wanted to be able sincerely to admire himself: hence Stendhal's repeated insistence on the emperor's evident displeasure when he came to realize that he had allowed himself to resort to a political expedient that he found shameful. Stendhal's various fictional hero(in)es all spend a great deal of time attempting to live up to their ideas of themselves in this way – just as Stendhal himself spent most of his adult life trying to live up to his idea of himself. As Simone de Beauvoir points out, in the exemplary case of Mathilde de la Mole, 'the esteem she has for herself [is] dearer to her than her own life.'[1]

Stendhal's false ambition of 1811 quickly led to his appointment to work alongside Vivant Denon on Napoleon's looted art collection for the purposes of establishing the Musée Napoléon – subsequently the Louvre. Working with so much Italian art brought Stendhal back to the idea of writing. In the autumn of the same year, now back in Italy, he bought Luigi Lanzi's *Storia pittorica dell'Italia* (it has a much longer title, but you get the general idea; 1796) – which he thought about translating into French – and began assembling materials for a historical work of his own on Italian art. In 1812, thus including his time on the road to and from Moscow, he started writing what would become the *Histoire de la peinture en Italie*. He kept going with this project, on and off, throughout 1813. In 1814, after the fall of Napoleon, after his own fall, after the Fall, all that remained to fill the days were his literary projects. But he still had not entirely shaken off the idea of outsourcing at least some of his writing.

Henri Beyle's first published work – the *Vies de Haydn, de Mozart et de Métastase* (it too has a much longer title, 1815) – was written in 1814, while Stendhal was still in Paris, shamelessly and ineffectually rallying to the restored monarchy of Louis XVIII in the hope of continuing in employment as the sole plausible means of staving off bankruptcy. Beyle modestly hid behind a deliberately absurd pseudonym, Louis-Alexandre-César Bombet, which was just as well, as he hadn't himself written that much of his first published book. The bulk of the 'Life of Haydn' had in fact been derived from a work by Giuseppe Carpani, who of course owes his own posthumous fame entirely to Stendhal's whimsical decision to plagiarize him. Carpani proved in no way grateful for the honour done to him, protesting furiously in print once he had spotted Bombet's larceny; first Bombet's imaginary brother and then the fabled Bombet himself brazenly riposted, also in print. Stendhal seems to have found the entire incident funny. He would go on, throughout the rest of his writing life, to appropriate ideas, facts and sentences from a variety of sources, sometimes with the permission of the author, sometimes crediting the original authors, sometimes plagiarizing. It has been argued that Stendhal's plagiarisms were an extension of the synthesizing method he had been taught to adopt when compiling reports for the Ministry of War. Certainly, a number of Stendhal's non-fiction texts set out to offer their reader a *précis* or loose translation of existing material, enlivened by his running commentary. The *Vies de Haydn, de Mozart et de Métastase* set out, in very large part, simply to plagiarize. A lot of the things Stendhal did were probably construed in his own mind as jokes for his private entertainment, typically with himself as the punchline. Equally, he may well have been at times quite dishonest, fascinated as he was by questions of sincerity and truth.

Stendhal's two next works were the finally completed *Histoire de la peinture en Italie* (1817), credited to M.B.A.A. (Monsieur Beyle Ancien Auditeur [Mr Beyle, the former auditor]), and *Rome, Naples et Florence en 1817* (1817), attributed at last to M. de Stendhal, a Prussian cavalry officer taking a well-earned holiday in the Italian peninsula. Both works exhibited considerably more originality than the *Vies de Haydn, de Mozart et de Métastase*, in their content, certainly (some understandable borrowings from Lanzi in the *Histoire de la peinture en Italie* notwithstanding), but more importantly also in their tone – Stendhal's tone is everything when it comes to our engagement with his works. Aside from the two extremely famous novels, he wrote another three novels that turn out to be just as interesting in their own various ways as the two that are famous, as well as the *Vie de Henry Brulard* and a small number of memorably disconcerting short stories. It is hard to imagine anyone reading either the *Histoire de la peinture en Italie* or *Rome, Naples et Florence en 1817* today were it not for the fact that they happen to have been written by the author of *Le Rouge et le Noir* and *La Chartreuse de Parme*. Equally, *Le Rouge et le Noir* and *La Chartreuse de Parme* could never have been written were it not for Stendhal's Milanese interlude and his publications of this period, as well as such abortive side-projects as the *Vie de Napoléon*. He had begun this last work on 28 May 1817, inspired by a synoptic biography of the emperor that had appeared in the Wikipedia of the Romantic era that was the *Edinburgh Review*. Stendhal had only recently discovered this incredibly useful publication, in September 1816. Immediately it helped reshape his view of Romanticism as something not so much German as Byronic. Stendhal's fictions would owe a lot not only to the *Edinburgh Review* but to his evenings spent discussing modern ideas with Ludovico di

Anonymous artist, presumed portrait of Angela Pietragrua, 19th century.

Breme, the man who had in fact introduced him to this journal, as well as to Milan's leading liberals (Monti, Pellico) and the distinguished foreigners (Byron, Hobhouse, Lord Brougham) who would drop by to see them.

The *Vie de Napoléon* functioned at first simply as a translation, then eventually as a reworking of the biography in the *Edinburgh Review*. Stendhal abandoned it in March 1818, but in June of that same year he returned to it, this time with a view to turning it into a riposte to Mme de Staël's attacks on Napoleon in her posthumous – and to Stendhal's mind libellous (*N*, p. 15) – *Considérations sur les principaux événements de la Révolution française* (Considerations on the Principal Events of the French Revolution, 1818). Given that Milan's liberals all revered Mme de Staël, this project was hardly calculated to serve his interests – Stendhal would go on to make a career of shocking his acquaintances with outlandish opinions, which he half believed and which he justifiably considered to be very funny, particularly given the absurd humourlessness of his audience. One of his insights about the modern world is that we all take ourselves far too seriously as we parade our opinions and otherwise pointlessly posture.

Stendhal's later fictions owe most, however, not to the *Edinburgh Review* or to the circle of Milanese and other intellectuals that gathered round di Breme, but rather to the two women who together came to dominate his life between the end of his Napoleonic adventure and his expulsion by the Austrians in 1821. Stendhal's return to Milan naturally saw him renew his relationship with Angela Pietragrua, 'a sublime harlot [*catin sublime*] in the Italian manner' (*OI*, II, p. 545).

His private names for her were Lady Simonetta, after the Villa Simonetta in Milan, and Gina, hence Gina Sanseverina in *La Chartreuse de Parme*, which would suggest that he continued to consider her sublime almost a quarter of a century after their relationship had collapsed – it is for this reason that Jean Prévost likewise categorizes Gina Sanseverina not as an Amazon but as a sublime harlot. Angela's private name for him was 'the Chinaman'. She was never what one might call besotted by Stendhal – in 1811, she had not at first been able to recollect the unimportant young acquaintance of 1800 and he had therefore been forced to reintroduce himself. In 1814, she could at least still remember who he was, but seemed to find him less appealing now that he had lost his position and almost all of his money. He nevertheless considered himself to be in love with her, as he had been in 1811, and as he had been in 1800 – she possessed his 'admiration' and 'almost' his 'passion' for he considered her character to be 'sublime and tender' (*OI*, I, p. 759). In all of her various insincere guises, Stendhal consistently identifies Angela (Gina) as sublime.

Stendhal was demonstrating, once again, the constancy of his intermittent affections: remaining true to his own former emotions mattered enormously to him, his reputation among his friends for inconsistency and unpredictability notwithstanding. Angela appears to have cared about remaining true to her former emotions a good deal less – understandably so, for Stendhal was not an attractive man. Less understandably, though, she appears to have now taken a certain amount of pleasure from exerting emotional control over her portly lover. Their relationship appears to have been founded, in this period at least, on an absolute agony of lies, slights and humiliations, all of them visited by Angela on Stendhal. Either she was bent on avenging her sex, which would make a lot of sense normally, but somehow seems unlikely in this particular case, or she had a narcissistic personality disorder. Stendhal's jottings, some of them in the Franglais he reserved for the coded expression of his most doleful moments, reveal just how pathetically he found himself in her thrall at this already low point in his life. '*She* déclare *to me our* rupture' (*OI*, I, p. 917), he notes on 16 October 1814. That same day, he writes in his journal that 'having not written to her from Genoa for an entire fortnight, she has informed me that all is over between us. She says the spell is broken' (*OI*, I, p. 916). Was there ever a spell? Probably not. On 11 December, they are back to having dinner. For the rest of the month, Stendhal mournfully reverts to his version of English, recording himself as having been '*crossed in love*' (*OI*, I, p. 922), in a state of '*unhappy love*' (*OI*, I, p. 923) and '*mad by love*' (*OI*, I, p. 924). '*I am loving*,' he records in another marginal note on 20 December (*OI*, I, p. 924). On 26 December he finally accepts that she didn't, in fact, love him (no really). On 1 January 1815, he notes that, for the first time since 20 December, he managed to do some work. By 6 January, he was back to feeling '*mad by love*' (*OI*, I, p. 928). And so on.

Angela probably did have a narcissistic personality disorder, in which case she had found the perfect victim in Stendhal: as has already been noted, he had an obsessive fear of being duped, which, naturally enough, held him transfixed when very plainly being duped by someone to whom he had chosen to give his trust. This pattern emerges slightly differently, to even more devastating effect, in the most important of his affective relationships. Angela continued to run rings round an increasingly despondent and irresolute Stendhal for almost all of 1815. On 14 January that despondency had further intensified when he learnt of the death of Alexandrine Daru. He promptly decided to dedicate the *Histoire de la peinture en Italie* to her sacred memory – he had hitherto planned to dedicate it to Angela. Despite his grief at the loss of a woman he had loved and, needless to say, continued to love, he remained desperate to make his relationship with Angela work – it was this desperation that she ruthlessly exploited. They continued to have sex, but ever more sporadically and ever more transparently as a function of his cash gifts to her. Almost everything Angela said to him as they chugged along, so unhappily on his side, appeared deliberately calculated to be recognized by Stendhal as a lie. 'Love has died' (*OI*, I, p. 947), he notes bleakly on 15 October. 'Is it not better to be duped in this way than no longer to care?' (*OI*, I, p. 948), he asks himself hopefully a day later. Their definitive parting was, by this stage, inevitable.

The control exerted by Angela lay in her calculation that Stendhal would not be able to openly acknowledge her words as lies for fear of being forced to give her up forever. All this eventually became clear to Stendhal, in hindsight: 'Lady Sim[onetta] went to an enormous amount of trouble to lose Dom[ini]que, duping him a thousand times. Her loss is immense. She would otherwise have had him for life' (*OI*, I, p. 961). It was inexplicable to him, though, why she didn't place more value on the sincerity of his esteem and the constancy of his affection. The final crisis in their relationship is recounted in some detail by Mérimée, who both misconstrues and gives us an insight into the lessons that Stendhal himself derived from this lamentable episode in his affective life.

Stendhal's fictions suggest that he thought of male heterosexual desire, in its passionate form, as a successful reading of female desire and a sharing in it – it is perhaps because Octave de Malivert cannot read Armance's evident sexual desire for him that he finds it impossible to perform sexually with her, although there are numerous other theories as to why this might prove to be the case. Passion, for Stendhal, was the sexual form of empathy – dispassionate desire was, by contrast, simply something to be gratified, often by means of a financial transaction. To this extent, Stendhal's various male protagonists experience their passion only as a feedback effect of the genuinely autonomous and anarchic female desire that Stendhal repeatedly posits in his fictions. Likewise, what mattered to Stendhal was whether Angela found him attractive, or rather whether she esteemed him sufficiently to forget about his physical shortcomings – always self-conscious about his portliness, Stendhal would eventually write to Pauline, during the retreat from Moscow in 1812, that 'I've lost everything and own only the clothes I am wearing. In much better news, I'm now thin' (*CG*, II, p. 397). Stendhal valued Angela's desire for him precisely because it appeared anarchic, and therefore both sincere and unpredictable. Mostly she found him ugly, naming him the Chinaman as a means of reminding him that neither his features nor his complexion conformed to classical standards of European beauty. But at other times, she suddenly seemed to find him attractive, and it is this changeability that appears to have held him long in her thrall. Even though he defined his own feelings for her in terms of constancy, he liked to posit her feelings for him

Achille Devéria (1800–1857), *Prosper Mérimée*, 19th century, lithograph.

as charmingly erratic. But did she have any feelings for him at all? *That is the question*, as Stendhal might have put it – he was fond of portentous, cod-Shakespearean forays into English at moments of high emotion (and perplexity). Mérimée certainly didn't think Angela had any feelings for him.

From the author of *Carmen*'s perspective, Angela revealed herself to Stendhal as lying, manipulative, inconstant and constitutionally incapable of sincerely returning his male desire: 'For all the good faith of Italian women, which he would endlessly contrast with the coquetry of French women, Mme Grua was always betraying him shamefully' (*HB*, p. 450). She betrayed Stendhal definitively and incontrovertibly by having enthusiastic sex with another man while completely unaware that Stendhal was, in fact, observing her from inside a cupboard. She had made this huge song and dance about giving herself to him, and now here she was happily giving herself to another with no fuss whatsoever. Very plainly, her treachery was unforgivable.

A more subtle observer than Mérimée might have understood that it was not Angela's infidelity that had left Stendhal so hurt, but rather the prior control that she had exerted by claiming to love him even as she flaunted her evident lack of goodwill, thereby ruthlessly exploiting his obvious emotional need to believe in her. What is striking, however, is Stendhal's refusal to fall back either on misogyny or a detached understanding of her controlling narcissism to explain away Angela's behaviour. Stendhal was a generous man, who refused to reframe his relationships with the people he admired in terms of reductive narratives. This is what Mérimée has to say about Stendhal's reaction to the discovery of Angela's faithlessness, or rather her bad faith, of the previous months:

> B[eyle] told me that the singularity of what he was witnessing and the absurdity of the situation had initially struck him as insanely funny, and that he had found it incredibly difficult not

to alarm the guilty pair by suddenly laughing out loud. It was only a little later that he came to feel his misfortune. His faithless lover, against whom he had avenged himself only by lightly mocking her, tried to make him relent by going down on her knees and begging his forgiveness, before crawling after him in this posture from one end of a long gallery to the other. Pride had prevented him from forgiving her, and he regretted this bitterly, remembering how passionate she had looked. Never had he found her so attractive; never had she been so in love with him. His pride had induced him to sacrifice the greatest pleasure the two of them could ever have shared together. It took him eighteen months to recover. (*HB*, pp. 450–51)

At the moment of discovery, Angela had suddenly felt her irrevocable loss. She had only been playing a spiteful game: the instinctive aim had been casually to torture Stendhal, not to lose him. And now, suddenly, anarchically, sincerely, she desired him, he could read her desire, and in the reading of that desire found himself desiring her. Never had he found her so attractive, for never had she been so in love with him. The greatest pleasure they could ever have shared together does not necessarily mean sex, although sex would doubtless have occurred had he forgiven her: it means two people for a moment no longer feeling radically alone, as Stendhal was prone always to feeling on account of his former childhood isolation and as Angela was prone always to feeling on account of her raging narcissism. It would have done them both a power of good to have shared that moment and put all her lies behind them. Instead, Stendhal spent eighteen months prostrated by grief: "'I was stupefied", he said. "I could no longer think. I felt trapped under an unbearable weight, without really being able to make sense of my feelings. It's the worst thing in the world; it robs you of all your energy.'" (*HB*, p. 451)

The lessons that Stendhal derived from this episode and, more particularly, his subsequent regret and prostration, were lessons of generosity and forgiveness. He should have forgiven her for not desiring him (for why should she have?) as well as for desiring others (for why shouldn't she have?). He should have been suitably grateful to her for those few occasions when she had in fact desired him, not least because it was only through her desire that he had managed to experience direct desire as he understood this.

It is against the background provided by his long pursuit of Angela, and his sacrifice to his own stupid pride of the happiness they could still have shared, that we should read Stendhal's long pursuit of Metilde Dembowski, née Viscontini, also known as Matilde, Mathilde or Métilde – this last version of her name being the one most favoured by Stendhal and so most commonly used by Stendhalians. She would appear as Léonore in *De l'Amour* before giving her name and maybe some aspects of her personality to the wonderful Mathilde de La Mole.

Stendhal fell in love with Métilde on 4 March 1818. He looks back on this event – using his best Franglais, with some 'Fritalien' thrown in for extra intensity – in a note of 10 June 1819:

> *The greatest event of his life*:
> 4 March 1818, visite à M. *who pleases to me*.
> 30 September 1818, *nel Giardino* (*OI*, II, p. 33)

She was so important to Stendhal that he seems never to have told Mérimée about her, hence the latter's misprision that Angela Pietragrua and Clémentine Curial were Stendhal's only 'passionate loves' (*amours-passions*, *HB*, p. 449). Stendhal writes about Métilde both in English and in the third person, not in order to create psychological or critical distance, but rather in order, paradoxically, to create a paroxysm of intimacy – for Stendhal, we are never more ourselves than when writing in another language in the third person.

Métilde was 28 and separated from a Napoleonic army officer of Polish descent, whom she had married in 1807 and with whom she

Anonymous artist, presumed portrait of Matilde Dembowski, 19th century.

had two sons. She was an Italian patriot and therefore disapproved of her husband's attempts to rally to the Austrian cause after the first fall of the Emperor. He was in any case a physically and psychologically abusive husband. In July 1814 she therefore decided to escape the marriage by leaving Milan for Bern, taking her youngest son with her. She returned to Milan in June 1816 and fled again after further clashes with her husband, before returning definitively in November of that same year. Métilde was a brave and angry woman, as jealous of her own freedom as she was of the freedom of her city and her people. For Stendhal, she came to define what it was to be 28: fully adult, unbowed and generous; that is, not a narcissist.

In the *Vie de Henry Brulard*, Henry refers to this period in his life as follows: 'Métilde occupied my life absolutely from 1818 to 1824. And I'm not cured yet . . . having just spent a good quarter of an hour or so thinking just about her. Did she love me?' (*OI*, II, p. 532) The answer to that question almost certainly is no. It is clear what Stendhal found attractive about Métilde: he admired her for her courage and her political idealism; he was drawn to her Italian passion; he thought her generous; he thought her sincere and past caring what others thought of her; he found her extremely physically attractive. Métilde, by contrast, appears to have thought of Stendhal as weird – he would have preferred 'singular'. His letters to her from this period repeatedly fend off accusations of 'indelicacy' and 'disrespect' (*CG*, III, pp. 206, 210, 215).

Stendhal spent a great deal of time trying to show Métilde the person that he was. This process was intended as an exciting voyage of discovery for them both but, increasingly, she resented him for the importunity of his self-revelations. Nevertheless, she appears, at least, to have noticed some of his very real qualities of intelligence, wit and sincerity, enough, occasionally, to soften her otherwise brutal rejection of his advances and so inadvertently to give him hope. She offered him someone to believe in for the rest of his life.

Stendhal's attempts to seduce Métilde involved a great deal of helplessly telling her how wonderful she was. Like Gros before her, she appears not to have liked what she heard. Stendhal's letter of 12 May 1819 (*CG*, III, p. 206) captures the tenor of his lovelorn prose: 'In your presence, I'm as timid as a child and the words die on my lips: I can only look at you and admire you. Must I think of myself as falling so far short of who I truly am – as being so dull?'

Next to 'so dull', Stendhal adds a note, again in Franglais: 'Voici le naturel *of this man*' (*CG*, III, p. 206). For Stendhal, love – and for that matter, friendship – proceeds from our natural state: our willingness to admit to ourselves, and generously to show to others, the poor saps we in fact are, rather than the splendid personages we waste so much time endeavouring to project. It is this willingness to reveal the self that also characterizes Stendhalian generosity. One cannot be 28 without it. Sadly, though, the more we come to terms with our lack of prepossession, the less it is possible to believe that we could ever attract desire – happily, past a certain age, we are not going to attract desire anyway, a thought Stendhal appears to have found consoling.

Stendhal's off-off relationship with Métilde can perhaps best be understood by the catastrophe that unfolded in Volterra between 3 and 10 June 1819. Métilde had left Milan on 12 May, the same day that Stendhal wrote the lovelorn letter just cited. She formally forbad him from following her, her intention being to spend time with her two children and, anyway, plainly having had enough of him. In a characteristic agony of uncertainty as to what Métilde was trying to tell him, he spent the days that followed '*thinking to* M.' (*OI*, II, p. 32) until he could take it no longer: on 24 May, he fatefully resolved to follow her and find out once and for all whether she intended to embark on a passionate affair with him. She did not.

Volterra is not so much enchanting as austerely forbidding. Certainly, Stendhal must have found it so when he arrived on 3 June. There is a fairly obvious walk to take through the centre of town: Stendhal took it and immediately spotted Métilde, but managed to avoid being seen in his turn. Around eight o'clock that same evening, he was not so lucky.

Stendhal's alleged intention in making the trip had been simply to breathe the same air as his beloved; he appears to have deluded himself that he could avoid detection with the help of a pair of green-tinted spectacles. She was not pleased. If she could have stabbed him in a bath, she would no doubt have done so – it is possible women were most attractive to Stendhal not, in fact, when they themselves suddenly desired him, but rather when they were in a murderous rage. Stendhal tried to explain himself, in a long letter of 11 June and then again in a long letter of 30 June.

A brief correspondence in July and August appeared to signal a thaw. Thereafter, he lived in the hope of seeing her here and there for a few minutes, as on 5 April 1820 and then again on 17 April 1820. He saw her for the last time on 7 June 1821, at his request. The Austrians and the Italian liberals had, in their turn, become suspicious of Stendhal. What was he doing in Milan? Was he a spy? Was he a revolutionary? It was time for him to leave before being arrested, expelled or ostracized. All he could think about was that this meant leaving Métilde behind, never to see her again. His thoughts immediately turned to suicide:

> I left Milan for Paris on the [blank] June 1821, I think carrying the sum of 3,500 francs, finding consolation only in the thought that I'd blow my brains out once that sum was exhausted. After three years of intimacy [really?], I was leaving behind a woman I adored, who loved me [really?], and who never gave herself to me [really]. Even after all these years, I'm no closer to understanding the motives for her conduct . . . Perhaps one day, when I'm very old and have cooled considerably, I'll have the courage to speak of the years 1818, 1819, 1820 and 1821.
>
> In 1821, I had a great deal of trouble resisting the temptation to blow my brains out. I drew a pistol in the margins of a bad romantic drama I was cobbling together at the time [. . .] I think my eagerness to find out what would happen politically prevented me from putting an end to my days; perhaps, without realizing it, I was also afraid of the physical pain. (*oi*, ii, p. 432)

Another thing keeping him alive was *De l'Amour*, the book he had decided, on 29 December 1819, to write as a way of dispassionately thinking through what happens to us when we fall in love, and of passionately reliving what had happened to him when he had fallen in love with Léonore, Métilde, Matilde, Mathilde. Maybe when the 3,500 francs ran out, he would continue to write about love as a way of making what sense he could of Métilde's inexplicable shows of indifference. The first of those novels would be *Armance*, a deliberately frustrating text about frustration.

6

Restoration: *Armance*, 1821–7

Stendhal returned to Paris in 1821 with the same elusive goal in the back of his mind as when he had returned to Milan in 1814: to rediscover the freedom he had first experienced in the rue d'Angivillers in 1803. But he was too much in turmoil readily to perceive this aim. Instead, his thoughts continued to turn around his grim curiosity as to how political events would unfold – the Restoration being surely doomed to fail – and around his lingering wish to blow his brains out. It was this confluence of ideas that led him briefly to entertain a course of action even more drastic than his suicide.

Stendhal was a very odd kind of Romantic. Octave de Malivert, the (anti-)hero of his first novel, *Armance*, kills himself by secretly taking poison and then pretending to die of natural causes while travelling to Greece ostensibly to emulate, but actually only superficially to imitate, Byron – the latter had of course died in Missolonghi in 1824, not poetically fighting the Ottomans but prosaically succumbing to fever and sepsis. This course of (in)action makes Octave quite a conventional Romantic hero: he's self-defeatingly and self-pityingly ambivalent both about his participation in society and about his relationship with the woman he simultaneously loves and rejects, all in the manner of Chateaubriand's René, Constant's Adolphe, Duras' Olivier and so on. In Stendhalian terms, however, Octave is no kind of hero at all, for he merely deludes himself that he is following in

Byron's footsteps: Byron doesn't kill himself as part of a compulsive strategy of avoidance; rather, he happens to die while trying to impart meaning to his life, the way Stendhal's hero(in)es, Octave apart, each try to impart meaning to theirs. Stendhal knew Byron personally just about well enough – he had very briefly met him, and anyway read about him in the *Edinburgh Review* – actually to have liked and admired him. By comparison, Octave is a very poor sap indeed. In 1821, however, Stendhal was a poor sap also. His eventual clear-eyed account of Octave's vulnerability and self-loathing is therefore founded just as much on identification and empathy as it is on detached amusement. But Stendhal wasn't only a sap in 1821: he was trying to impart meaning to his life, if necessary by imparting meaning to his death.

Stendhal discusses all of this himself. In the *Souvenirs d'égotisme* (1832), he offers the following layered account of his state of mind:

'The most terrible of misfortunes', I exclaimed to myself, 'would be if the male friends amongst whom I now live, themselves so cold, were to guess at my passion, and for a woman I've never had!'
I told myself this in June 1821 and can see now for the first time, as I write these words in June 1832, that this fear of mine, which I must have repeated to myself a thousand times, was in fact the guiding principle of my life for a decade. It's as a result of this fear that I became a wit. (*OI*, II, p. 434)

The reference to not having 'had' Métilde is an example of Stendhal's habitual free indirect discourse, as revealed by the exclamation mark: this is not his opinion but the likely opinion of his cold – the French is, in fact, *sec* (dry) – male friends. What he feared was their all-too-predictable cynicism: *What? All this fuss over a woman, and now you're telling me you haven't even slept with her?* It is in the light of this fear that we should read both his not telling Mérimée about Métilde and the former's reports of his friend's alleged attitude to women.

Stendhal did not necessarily tell his male friends what he was really thinking. Instead he tried to amuse them with his wit, as a way of hiding his true feelings and in the hope of thus preserving them inviolate. One of his favourite jokes was to feed his male friends their own opinions in exaggerated form, thereby both scandalizing and confusing them. 'God gave us language to hide our thoughts' (*ORC*, I, [*Le Rouge et le Noir*]). Stendhal eventually became a very funny man on the Parisian social scene as a way of concealing both his unhappy passion for Métilde and his resulting desire to blow his brains out, but not until the winter of 1826: 'before then, I'd remain quiet out of laziness' (*OI*, II, p. 541). George Sand, who met him travelling on a steamer from Lyon to Marseille in 1833, offers the following impressions of meeting Stendhal in her *Histoire de ma vie* (The Story of My Life, 1854–5):

He was brilliantly witty and his conversation reminded me of that of [the novelist and journalist Henri de] Delatouche, only less delicate and graceful, but more penetrating. At first glance, he was also like Delatouche physically: fat, with very fine features under all the puffiness of his face. But Delatouche was rendered beautiful, from time to time, by sudden melancholy, whereas Beyle's expression remained satirical and mocking at all times. [...] Above all, he affected disdain for all types of vanity and endeavoured to uncover some form of pretention in each of his interlocutors in order to subject it to the sustained fire of his mockery. But I do not believe that he was unkind: he tried far too hard to appear so [...] We separated [...] after several days of jovial conviviality; but, given that the back of his mind betrayed a taste for obscenity, whether in his habits or his dreams, I confess that I'd had enough of him.[1]

Sand never fully penetrated the back of Stendhal's mind, thrown off, for example, by the 'somewhat grotesque and not at all pretty'

Newspaper reproduction of a sketch of Stendhal dancing drunkenly in a tavern, by George Sand's lover Alfred de Musset (1810–1857).

spectacle of watching him dance drunkenly around the table in a tavern.[2] She understood that he was making mock by his outlandish behaviour, but not the sentiments that underpinned that mockery. In this, she was little different to his friends. Most of these friends Stendhal had known since his school days: Romain Colomb (the eventual executor of his will), Louis Crozet, Louis Barral, Édouard

Mounier, Félix Faure. He distanced himself from these last two as they advanced in their political careers and defended policies he considered to be ethically unacceptable, but generally Stendhal's friendships, including with his former lovers, are striking for their longevity. In the 1820s Stendhal acquired an additional circle of close and trusted friends: Destutt de Tracy, the painters Gérard and Delacroix, the naturalist Georges Cuvier, Giuditta Pasta, Mérimée, Adolphe de Mareste, the Neapolitan exile Domenico Fiore and the English liberal Sutton Sharpe. The men in this group, especially Mérimée and Mareste, tended to laugh at overt displays of emotion. As a result, Stendhal would reveal what he was really thinking much more often to his female friends, with whom he was really quite warm, and even, on grand occasions, moist (in his words, *humide*): Stendhal was prone to emotivity, sincerity and tears. He wanted, at all costs, to protect this aspect of himself: allow himself to continue feeling something for his fellow human beings so that, when the opportunity arose, he could still make meaningful connections with the likewise sincere – we few, we happy few, we band of brothers and sisters. This is the meaning of the ending of *Lucien Leuwen*, which sees Lucien travel to take up a post in Italy while succumbing to 'tender melancholy' and 'a state of emotion and sensitivity to the slightest things', before lecturing himself, in the novel's final sentence, on the need 'to adopt a seemly degree of aloofness towards the people he was about to meet' (*ORC*, II, p. 716). Stendhal wanted to find a special language with which to not hide his thoughts from the people he trusted and, mostly, these people were women. The rest of the time, he wore a cold mask of impassivity.

To return to Stendhal's own account of his state of mind in June 1821, he clearly felt himself to be very isolated, far from the woman and the friends and the city that he loved:

I entered Paris and found it worse than ugly – an insult to my despair. I had only one idea in my head: *not to allow my thoughts*

to be discovered. After a week in the political vacuum of Paris,
I told myself: 'Take advantage of my despair to k[ill] L[ouis] 18.'
(*OI*, II, p. 434)

Find out what the next political development would be? Check.
End it all? Check. But how serious was Stendhal? Probably not
enough to have produced a detailed plan of action; probably enough
to have spent entire minutes at a time convinced that he would go
through with the assassination of France's elderly, obese, in all senses
impotent, restored monarch. In 1820 Louvel's assassination of the
Duc de Berry, Louis XVIII's heir and seemingly the last plausible
continuator of the Bourbon line, had no doubt reminded Stendhal
of his childhood fascination for tyrannicides. Why not go out with
a splash like Charlotte Corday? Certainly it would have been easy
enough to kill Louis XVIII, even just on the spur of the moment: he
was often to be seen patiently sitting in his carriage as it was being
pulled along at a stately pace through the streets of Paris.

Killing himself by first killing Louis XVIII would not only have
hastened the demise of the Bourbon line, but served as a wonderful
red herring: had Stendhal acted, who would ever have guessed that
his true object would in fact have been to escape the relentless grief
produced by his definitive loss of Métilde? Certainly none of his
male friends. In the end, though, Stendhal decided not to kill Louis
XVIII, but instead to visit England.

On his journey, Stendhal stopped off in a tavern in Calais,
where a drunk English sea captain insulted him. Stendhal failed
to realize the seriousness of the incident until his travelling
companion, a memorably blond Englishman unimprovably
named Edward Edwards, told him he ought to have challenged
his antagonist to a duel:

I'd already made this horrible error once before, in Dresden, in
1813, when dealing with M [blank], who subsequently went mad.

I do not lack for bravery; such a thing could no longer happen
to me now. But, in my youth, when I improvised I was mad
[. . .] Mr Edwards's intervention had the same effect on me
as the cock crowing had on St Peter. (*oi*, ii, p. 476)

Stendhal clearly takes his failure in Calais extremely seriously, so
seriously in fact that he misremembers when it occurred. Edwards
had in fact been his travelling companion in 1817, when he had first
spent two weeks in London, and not in 1821 when he was escaping
Paris and the prying eyes of his friends. There is a reason for the slip
of memory: Stendhal's failure to challenge the English sea captain
to a duel is emblematic of his state of mind not in 1817, when he
still felt relatively jaunty, but in 1821, when he had fallen apart.
The *Souvenirs d'égotisme* are all about the decade it took him to
pull himself back together. Put another way, they are all about his
succumbing to emotion and trying to restore himself to reason. *De
l'Amour* had similarly been written with the idea of establishing the
critical distance that might allow him to survive the collapse of his
last remaining hopes with regard to Métilde, by proving to himself
that his feelings for her were, in fact, so many symptoms of a human
affliction; that his love for her was, in fact, what might today be
labelled limerence – an involuntary state of adoration producing
obsessive thoughts, rapid swings from euphoria to despair and
the strong desire to have one's feelings reciprocated. But Stendhal
was sufficiently Romantic to believe that what he felt for Méthilde
was more than the disordered state of mind he dispassionately set
out to describe as though he were simply an Ideologue – however
ridiculous, delusional or weird, his sentiments were also noble,
disinterested and true. It is Stendhal's awareness of complexity
– his own and that of others – and his refusal to reframe human
beings in terms of reductive narratives that prompted him
to write *Armance*, perhaps the least understood and least
understandable French novel of the nineteenth century.

For the time being, Stendhal was still prudently holed up in London. He went to the theatre and generally overdosed on Shakespeare as a way of communing with Métilde. A couple of his friends, Mareste and Rémy Lolot, were also in town. To distract him, they decided to take Stendhal to a brothel. Already in Paris, some of his male friends had arranged for him to visit a prostitute in their company: he had not managed to perform sexually, despite or because of the extraordinary splendour of her person. 'In 1821, love gave me a very funny virtue: chastity' (*oi*, ii, p. 444). It is on the strength of this first Parisian episode that Stendhal enjoys his ongoing reputation for sexual dysfunction – the stupendously detailed surviving record of his relentless sexual activity notwith-standing. His decision to include a chapter entitled 'On Fiascos' in *De l'Amour* hasn't helped in this regard. Now, only a few months later, he once again found himself being dragged along on an expedition designed – but hardly calculated – to cheer him up. Yet, against all his expectations and despite his fear of further humiliation, Stendhal found the experience completely enchanting, as he recounts in the *Souvenirs d'égotisme*.

Miss Appleby and her two friends lived together on an equal footing in the smallest three-storey house Stendhal had ever seen. The young women, all very English with their chestnut hair, pallid skin and reserved manners, appeared embarrassed by the finery of their French visitors, just as Stendhal and Lolot appeared embarrassed by the indigence of their surroundings – in the end, Mareste had been too scared to come, fearing an ambush; it was only the possibility that the expedition would in fact end in an armed confrontation with a gang of English pimps that finally determined Stendhal and Lolot to embark on it. It turned out that Lolot being 'tall and fat' and Stendhal being 'fat', they could not bring themselves to sit on the tiny chairs: 'they seemed to have been made for dolls; we were scared of them giving way beneath us' (*oi*, ii, p. 484). An awkward silence ensued.

Remembering their duties as hosts, the young women offered to show their guests the garden. It was 7.5 metres (25 ft) long, 3 metres (10 ft) wide, and largely taken up by the basin in which they washed their clothes and a contraption that allowed them economically to brew their own beer. Lolot was disgusted and wanted to leave; Stendhal was touched and worried about humiliating the young women, now reduced to two in number. He lost his own sense that he would be either humiliated or assassinated and spent the night with Miss Appleby, who seemed quite alarmed by the number of weapons he had brought with him and insisted on turning down the light out of modesty. The following morning, Mareste was summoned to bring wine and food: this bounty was left to the two women and the two men promised they would return later that evening.

Stendhal thought of his impending reunion with Miss Appleby all day: he had lit upon the English phrase '*full of snugness*' (*OI*, II, p. 486) as a way of putting his new sensations of tranquillity into words. When he arrived with Lolot, he came bearing '*real champaign*', as the young women excitedly pointed out. When the cork popped, they expressed great happiness, in calm and measured tones: 'This was the first real and intimate form of consolation for the despair which poisoned my every moment alone. It's plain that I was only twenty in 1821.' (*OI*, II, p. 486)

Stendhal was in fact 38, but he was still sincere – not admirable, but sincere – in the manner of a much younger man. Miss Appleby eventually asked Stendhal if she could come to Paris with him – she apparently claimed she would eat only apples and cost him nothing. He thought about it and was deterred by memories of how difficult he had found it briefly living with his sister Pauline in 1816. It may in fact be Miss Appleby who, for a few minutes in 1821, came the closest to making Stendhal want to feel responsible for another human being. He really liked her and her company; he liked providing for her; but in the end, he didn't want to be responsible for anybody – it was a choice he had made for himself, at least after realizing that he would never be allowed to be a support to Métilde. Stendhal's conception of freedom worked both ways: he wanted himself to be free and assumed that everybody else wanted to be free also. He therefore ruled out formal ties with the people he loved, but that didn't stop him from loving those people. In a nutshell, this is Stendhal's conception of *égotisme*: it is what made him a warm and reliable person, full of good will and loyalty, and it is quite possibly why he never married or had children.

What Stendhal most liked about Miss Appleby was her complete lack of false airs: 'To my misfortune, I so dislike affectation that it's very difficult for me to be unaffected, sincere and good, or in other words perfectly German, when I'm with a French woman.' (*OI*, II, p. 488) Was Stendhal sincere with women? He loved their company; he loved their conversation; often, but not always, he wanted to sleep with them; typically, he admired them, far more so than he did men; he thought them capable of sincerity (as, for example, Métilde) but he also liked them when they were insincere (as, for example, Angela and eventually Alberthe de Rubempré) so long as they were magnificently insincere and not squalidly, self-servingly so. Perhaps, therefore, he recognized that he could himself be insincere with women, although, hopefully, only ever magnificently so, insincerity being sometimes to sincerity what literary fiction is to truth. Certainly, he remained all his thinking life aware of the grotesque imbalances of power and status between men and women, even as he often took advantage of these. Perhaps what Stendhal found touching about Miss Appleby was the patience with which she fought for a better life even as it must have been clear to her that the entire system was rigged against her, hence the sudden presence of a fat paying Frenchman in her bed.

Stendhal was more generally impressed, as well as appalled, by the patience of the English. He had never seen a people work so hard and for so little money; he had no idea why they did not rise up against their employers: 'The exorbitant and oppressive labour performed by the English worker avenges us for Waterloo and the four coalitions. At least we've now buried our dead and those of us who survive live happier lives than the English.' (*OI*, II, pp. 482–3)

Stendhal taught himself political economy on and off for most of his adult life, and in 1825 he even went so far as to write a political pamphlet attacking the French Industrialist lobby. His main contribution to the field was the thought that political economy focuses on economic prosperity and growth without giving any proper consideration to human happiness. Insofar as there is an argument for work – and Stendhal could see how it might make sense simply to loaf around in Naples looking at the view and soaking in the sun – that argument must concern itself with the happiness work procures us or the mental pain it spares us – from 1821 to 1832 work helped spare Stendhal the mental pain of thinking too much about Métilde. It is for this reason that he started contributing articles to the English and French press, published *De l'Amour*, produced a biography of Rossini, wrote two pamphlets in support of his idea of Romanticism, revised and added to *Rome, Naples et Florence* and wrote his first novel, *Armance*, all between 1822 and 1827. Equally, taking plentiful holidays spared him the mental pain of thinking too much about Métilde, who died on 1 May 1825, bringing their already off-off relationship to its final stage of nonexistence. '*Death of the author*', Stendhal noted in the margins of a copy of *De l'Amour* (*DA*, p. 422), putting Barthes and literary theory into their proper context. Always interested in the truth, Stendhal notes in the *Vie de Henry Brulard* that he recovered from her death really quite quickly, having already grieved for her so long in life: 'I preferred her dead to faithless; I wrote, I consoled myself, I was happy' (*OI*, II, p. 541).

Stendhal was fantastically good at finding ways to take leave, especially sick leave and unauthorized leave. It will be remembered that even his pseudonymous self was a cavalry officer on leave in Italy.

As we shall see, when he lived in Italy he in fact spent much of his time on leave in Paris. When he lived in Paris, he spent much of his time on leave in Italy or, as in 1821, in England. Adrift as Stendhal was after losing Métilde, he knew that he needed to continue to hunt for happiness and that he would probably most likely find it in unexpected places. For example, in London, and more especially in Richmond, he found that English trees made him happy. He liked the way they were planted asymmetrically and seemingly allowed to grow free (*oi*, ii, p. 478). All in all, London had proved an unexpected success.

Back in Paris in 1821, Stendhal tried to hide his melancholia with jokes. It turned out he was a funny man, and it was on that basis that he was allowed to make himself at home in literary and intellectual salons that without him continually ran the risk of listing into boredom. In 1822 he spent a lot of his evenings with his neighbour, Giuditta Pasta, in the rue de Richelieu, marvelling at the simplicity and generosity of one of the great operatic divas of the early nineteenth century. He also regularly attended the salon of one of his intellectual heroes, Destutt de Tracy, making friends with his family. He had first met Destutt in 1817, just after his return from that first trip to London: the great man spent fully an hour and ten minutes visiting Stendhal in his rooms and two days later sent him a copy of his latest book.

Destutt's salon proved attractive also because La Fayette, internationally famous ever since his emergence as a hero of the American War of Independence, was one of its leading lights:

> I immediately understood, without being told, that M. de La Fayette was quite simply a hero from Plutarch. He lived from day to day, not particularly intelligently, like Epaminondas performing the great deeds that presented themselves to him. (*oi*, ii, p. 455)

Michele Bisi (1788–1874), Giuditta Pasta as Desdemona in Rossini's *Otello*, 19th century, lithograph.

When not performing great deeds, La Fayette apparently filled his spare time pursuing inappropriately young women and mouthing the platitudes of a simplistic liberal politics. To the untrained eye, there didn't seem to be all that much to admire, but for Stendhal, 'accustomed to Napoleon and Lord Byron [let's allow him his poetic licence], and for that matter to Lord Brougham, Monti, Canova,

Rossini [he liked to pretend he'd met Rossini one day in an Italian inn: he hadn't], I immediately recognized M. de La Fayette's grandeur and that was enough for me' (*OI*, II, p. 456).

Retrospectively, Stendhal can see that he lived his life in this period 'from day to day', in the manner of La Fayette: 'I have always lived and live still from day to day, never thinking of what I shall do tomorrow' (*OI*, II, p. 440); 'I've never had enough good sense to arrange my affairs systematically. Chance has guided all my relationships' (*OI*, II, p. 489). Stendhal uses this narrative of a haphazard existence, governed only by chance, (not) to explain his life in the period after his return to Paris in 1821:

> Have I extracted the greatest possible happiness from the various situations in which chance has placed me over the course of the nine years I've just spent in Paris? What kind of man am I? Am I possessed of good sense? Is my good sense accompanied by penetration? Is my intelligence remarkable? Truth be told, I've no idea. Affected emotionally by what happens to me from day to day, I rarely give any thought to these fundamental questions, and when I do, my judgements vary according to my moods. My judgements are no more than fleeting insights. (*OI*, II, pp. 429–30)

The next paragraph shows why writing was the activity that finally consoled him for the loss of Métilde: 'let us see if, examining my conscience pen in hand, I'll manage to find something *positively* and *lastingly* true about myself' (*OI*, II, p. 430). Writing allowed him to make some sort of sense of the person he was: find the fictional narratives that alone could account for the past, and in particular the women he had loved: 'Most of these charming beings did not bestow their favours on me; but they literally occupied my entire life. They were succeeded by my writing' (*OI*, II, p. 542). Stendhal loved, and then he wrote, as his projected epitaph emphasized. Without the

Ary Scheffer, *Marquis de Lafayette*, 1823, oil painting.

narratives of his writing, it would have been as though he and his loves had never existed.

Stendhal allowed for the possibility that most people do not really exist, trapped in superficial and narcissistic narratives of the self that bear no relation to truth. He thought that, through writing and more especially through fiction, he could do better. In his life to date, he had been relatively pleased with himself, some mishaps such as the unfortunate incident in Calais apart. Like La Fayette, he had performed the great deeds, or at least the deeds, that circumstance had made possible for him. But writing gave him the chance to reflect on the five or six great questions that mattered to him and so to become fully adult: 'I cannot conceive of a man without at least some male energy, without ideas that are constant and profound, etc.' (*oi*, ii, p. 451).

One of these ideas related to what we might term 'female energy'. Just because he had lost Métilde doesn't mean he had lost his capacity to esteem women. In 1824 he started an affair with Countess Clémentine Curial, codename Menti, identified by him as the most intelligent of the women he had loved, just as Métilde had been the noblest in her sentiments (*oi*, ii, p. 545). He had first met her ten years earlier, at 6 a.m. on 18 March 1814, aged 26 and alluringly barefoot while dropping by to report the outcome of the battle of either Montmirail or Champaubert (in fact, the battle of Arcis-sur-Aube) to her anxious mother (*oi*, ii, p. 517). This had turned out to be the erotic highlight of that particular year. Menti had been quite taken with him too, or so it eventually turned out, for in 1824 she seduced him. He could hardly believe it. He tried 'not to let my soul become absorbed by the contemplation of her graces' (*oi*, ii, p. 780). He failed, and the result would be further heartache two years later: 'The astonishing victory with Menti didn't even give me a hundredth the pleasure than the pain she caused me by leaving me for M. de Rospiec' (*oi*, ii, p. 533):

What a year I passed from 15 September 1826 to 15 September 1827! The day of that horrific anniversary, I was on the island of Ischia, and I noticed a definite improvement: instead of thinking directly about my misfortune, as a few months earlier, I only remembered the melancholy in which I had been plunged in October 1826 for example. This observation consoled me greatly. (*OI*, II, p. 532)

One of the things Stendhal had loved about Menti was her tendency to defend him when he went too far with his jokes (*OI*, II, p. 635). This happened frequently, even before the winter of 1826 when, having lost Menti, he really could not have cared less about the consequences of what he said: 'I seemed atrocious to all those pygmies so diminished by the politeness of Paris' (*OI*, II, p. 464). Lots of the people who met him thought he was completely awful; the people he most liked in the entire world were the women who noticed that he was, in fact, joking.

At the end of 1826 Stendhal was back to square one: trying to get over Menti's rejection of him and trying to make jokes as a way of deflecting unwanted attention from his male friends. But he quickly moved to square two: in 1827, aged 44, Stendhal finally wrote a novel – one exclusively for the men and women who might possibly understand that he was, in fact, joking. The project was, in any case, intended to be parodic. Claire de Duras had written a succession of brief novels about thwarted love: love thwarted by racial difference (*Ourika*, 1824), love thwarted by class difference (*Édouard*, 1825) and love thwarted by erectile dysfunction (*Olivier ou le secret* (Olivier; or, The Secret), unpublished). As a self-proclaimed expert on the latter delicate topic, Stendhal decided to write his own novel with a view to publishing it anonymously and so implicitly passing it off as Duras' self-censored text. This intention was obscured by his choosing the title *Armance* and naming his anti-hero Octave rather than Olivier. It was further obscured by his only hinting

Anonymous artist, terracotta bust of Clémentine Curial, 19th century.

very subtly, if at all, at Octave's sexual impotence. The novel is a joke on its author in a variety of ways: it is a novel that sets out to frustrate its readers (a strange way to launch a career as a writer of fiction); it is a darkly comic novel about the poor sap that Stendhal had himself been in 1821, and had become again in the months that succeeded 15 September 1826; it is an attack on Romanticism written by an ostensible champion of the Romantic cause. The story tells of how a potentially impressive young man falls in love with an actually impressive young woman who very clearly reciprocates his feelings. Perversely, he misreads her, preferring his own paranoid narratives. He miscommunicates with her unaccountably over and over again until he despairs and finally kills himself. It is just as well that so few people read it at the time, given how incomprehensible they would likely have found it.

The novel exposes the problem of the near-impossibility of male heroism, while starting to explore the possibility of female heroism, in the France of the Restoration and indeed in the modern period ushered in by the fall of Napoleon. As its preface points out, the nineteenth century only started in 1815; arguably, we are still in that century: *Armance* is a novel about what it is to live amid the political, social and gender cleavages created by the French Revolution's brutal strangling at birth of women's rights, as finally enshrined in the Napoleonic code. Put another way, it is a novel about the Restoration, about the fraudulence of patriarchal authority and power. Put another way still, it is a novel about how the penis no longer works. *Armance* functions as a mirror held up to the French society of 1827. In 1829 Stendhal would write *Le Rouge et le Noir*, a novel that holds up a mirror to the France of 1830, but that also shows us what no mirror could ever fully capture.

7
Azure Skies: *Le Rouge et le Noir*, 1827–31

In *Le Rouge et le Noir*, the narrator sets up an unwieldy image to describe novels: apparently, they function like a mirror being hauled along a street on a cart. As the wheels of the cart hit a bump or pothole, the mirror jerks, so that sometimes it reflects the mud of the street and sometimes the azure skies. It is relatively easy to decode what the mud and the sky might symbolize: the mud is everything that is claggy, viscous, sordid and foul. For Balzac, mud is simply poverty; for Stendhal, it is the moral bankruptcy of a post-heroic age. By contrast, the azure skies represent the ideal in Stendhal, as pervasively in nineteenth-century poetry, azure having been the colour of the ideal since the Middle Ages, when it came to be associated with the Virgin Mary. He is asserting something that he says again in the second preface to *Lucien Leuwen*: 'the author believes that, except for the passion of the hero, the novel must function as a mirror' (*ORC*, II, p. 722). Stendhal's novels will show you the modern world as it is: the grubby place we still inhabit, with all its compromises and betrayals. The happy few are invited to reflect on the truthfulness of the reflection. But Stendhal's novels will also show you the heroism that still manifests itself in modern society, its one subsisting form of passion – by which Stendhal means both amorous passion and ethico-political passion. The happy few are invited to identify with the hero(in)es who exemplify this passion and, if possible, to emulate it in their own bids to hunt for happiness. The miserable many simply won't

Anonymous artist, *Alberthe de Rubempré*, 19th century.

understand: they will see themselves covered in mud and become angry or, as Stendhal puts it in the third preface to *Lucien Leuwen*, they will see only a reflection of their own livid faces and want to smash the mirror.

The colour azure also has a personal resonance for Stendhal. On 6 February 1829 he fell for Alberthe de Rubempré, codename Mme Azur. He had first met her a few days earlier: she was the 25-year-old cousin of Delacroix, by then one of Stendhal's circle of friends. 'For a month at most' (*OI*, II, p. 541), Stendhal was in love with Mme Azur, so named because she lived on rue Bleue and represented his ideal of female deportment, being foul-mouthed; fearless; committed to her own freedom, happiness and pleasure; and otherwise in no way what he liked to refer to as a 'Parisian doll' (*passim*). He thought of her as another Angela, only more heroic: 'Angela P[ietragrua] was a sublime harlot in the Italian manner, a Lucretia Borgia, and Mme Azur an unsublime harlot, a Du Barry' (*OI*, II, p. 545) – Du Barry was not a lady, and it is for this reason that Stendhal also antiphrastically referred to Alberthe as Lady Azur. The paradox Alberthe revealed to Stendhal was that one could be sublime by virtue of being intrepidly unsublime. It was a lesson that helped him to create both Mathilde de La Mole and Lamiel, two of the most obviously free female characters in nineteenth-century French literature, which otherwise tends to specialize in women as the trapped victims of men, society and circumstance.

A further paradox has already been touched upon: Stendhal invokes not Métilde but Alberthe as the woman he loved with a passion similar to the passion he felt for his mother. It is a commonplace of criticism to identify Mme de Rênal as maternal in *Le Rouge et le Noir* and Mathilde de La Mole as her opposite, yet Stendhal thought of his mother as he eventually thought of Mme Azur, not as some sort of Madonna but as an unchained gazelle: as a Mathilde or a Lamiel.

Stendhal in fact loved Alberthe for a bit longer than a month. For some four and a half months after first meeting her, he was unhappily obsessed by her, at least if his journal entries are anything to go by. For example, on 19 March 1829 he notes his melancholy as a result of her choosing to spend the evening with a certain To. A further entry uses an arcane mix of Latin and English to record his mounting distress: '*Dum legiebam she faciebat a time with* To. *Very melancholy*' (*OI*, II, p. 104). Literally, this means, 'While I was reading, she did one time with To. Very melancholy.' Less literally, it means, 'I tried to distract myself by reading but have just had the completely

unbearable thought that Alberthe must at this very moment be having sex with To. I want to die.' The entry for 2 April 1829 reads simply 'A storm, nerves, Azur' (*OI*, II, p. 105). Alberthe and Stendhal finally slept together on 21 June. On 28 July, they were still going strong, Alberthe having just demonstrated the sincerity of her own interest by rereading *Armance*. Henry Brulard's eagerness to minimize the importance of the relationship – also by affecting not to remember her actual name: 'Mme Azur, whose baptismal name I forget' (*OI*, II, p. 541) – suggests that he in fact doesn't want to talk about her because the subject exceeds what can be said. Instead, he would write about her in his fictions.

As the Restoration slid towards autocracy and the 1830 Revolution, Stendhal's thoughts turned to other azure skies also. Already in July 1827, *Armance* having been safely consigned to his publisher, he had set off on one of his periodic trips through Italy. The circuit was, by now, a familiar one. In Genoa, he met Alessandro Manzoni, who was in the process of becoming famous throughout Europe thanks to the success of *I promessi sposi* (The Betrothed, 1825–7); he proceeded to Leghorn, where he boarded a ship bound for Naples. There, he didn't see the city and die, but rather doubled back first to Rome and then Florence, where he met Alphonse de Lamartine, whose poetry had never made much of an

Attributed to Louis-Joseph Jay, 18th-century drawing long thought to be of Stendhal with his companions at the École Centrale, but actually of the Société Cipollésienne [the Society of the Onion], made up of French artists living in Rome at the time of the Restoration and attributed to Jean Alaux (1786–1864). Stendhal is allegedly seventh from the right.

impression on him but whom, to Stendhal's evident surprise, he now found he very much liked. December took him through Bologna, Ferrara and Venice. On 31 December he decided to try his luck and travelled to Milan, entering the city in the early hours of 1 January 1828 – for auld lang syne. The Austrian authorities immediately remembered expelling him as an undesirable liberal in 1821 and gave him twelve hours to leave the city.

By the end of January he was back in Paris, in the rue de Richelieu, where he remained until 1830. Much of this period was spent trying to imagine a gainful means of employment. He was a jobbing writer of biographies, nominally an expert in art, music, love and Italy. He was also a contributor of articles to the English press. It is not entirely clear how Stendhal first came to publish these articles in 1822, but he had gone on to produce a steady stream of them for the *Paris Monthly Review* (1822–5), *New Monthly Magazine* (1822–9) and *London Magazine* (1824–5). Now, having consulted with Sutton Sharpe as to its suitability, he started writing also for *The Athenaeum* (1828–9). Stendhal's articles for the English press appeared to confirm him as a jack of all trades, variously expert in French and other continental European literature, art, history, politics, science and philosophy. Mostly he contributed reviews of specific works or survey articles, although from time to time he would produce a series of more extended pieces sketching Parisian intellectual life. The time had come to specialize, and the specialism he chose was Italy. Much of the first half of 1828 was therefore spent compiling the voluminous *Promenades dans Rome* (Walks Through Rome, 1829), which did, in fact, eventually sell quite well – thanks in part to the sudden political interest created by the election of a new pope, Pius VIII, on 31 March 1829 – and established Stendhal's credentials as an authority on the peninsula. He was very good at giving the impression that he was in the know about all sorts of things, including, of course, the unknowable internal politics of the Vatican; his charm in fact lies in the way he just makes stuff up.

The *Promenades dans Rome* came out on 5 September; three days later, he left on another tour, this time around the southwest of France – Bordeaux, Toulouse, Carcassonne – and on to Barcelona (why not, given that he sometimes pretended M. de Stendhal had fought with the Napoleonic armies in Spain?), then back to Paris via Montpellier, Grenoble – it had to be done – and finally Marseille. It was in this last city – or possibly, in fact, in Chalon, for Stendhal may well have been lying either about the place or date where inspiration struck – that, in the early hours of 26 October 1829, Stendhal had the 'idea of *Julien*' (*ORC*, I, p. 960). Stendhal was about to become one of the major canonical authors of Western literature.

From this point on, some side projects such as the *Mémoires d'un touriste* (Memoirs of a Tourist, 1838) notwithstanding, Stendhal would, first and foremost, be a novelist and an autobiographer. If he put all his remaining energies into writing, indolent as he was by temperament, bored as he was by his eventual day job, and sick as he became, it is because at last he had found something he was superlatively good at doing, the indifference of the vast majority of his compatriots notwithstanding.

Le Rouge et le Noir tells the story of Julien Sorel, a young man of humble birth who rises first in provincial and then in Parisian society. Along the way, he is helped by a succession of surrogate father figures, each of whom identifies with him in some way, always mistakenly so. He is helped more especially by two aristocratic lovers, both of whom ascribe their own qualities to him. The first of these, Mme de Rênal, functions as a surrogate mother; the second, Mathilde de La Mole, as a surrogate sister. The novel seems to be about to end with Julien's successful assimilation into the ranks of the Restoration nobility, only for him to throw everything away by shooting Mme de Rênal as a punishment for her writing a letter to Mathilde's father denouncing him as a hypocrite who seduces aristocratic women in order to further his social ambitions. The novel ends with Mme de Rênal immediately forgiving Julien and Julien losing interest in Mathilde, for he now realizes that Mme de Rênal is in fact the love of his life. He is eventually condemned to death and executed. Mme de Rênal follows him to the grave three days later; Mathilde, pregnant with his child, survives.

Le Rouge et le Noir is the fruit of years of reflection on con artists and their marks. Put another way, it is the fruit of Stendhal's many years spent pondering empathy and narcissism. Fascinatingly, critics tend to ascribe narcissism in the novel to Mathilde, when, in fact, 'the idea of *Julien*' is probably the idea of producing an entirely new kind of male anti-hero, not passively emotive like Octave, but rather narcissistic and neurotic. None of the characters are what they first appear to be: the reader is told as much when introduced to Mme de Rênal and informed that she is the kind of person who 'could easily pass for stupid for the first fortnight of her acquaintance' (*ORC*, I, p. 381) – in no way is Mme de Rênal stupid, but rather by turns haughty and generous. Similarly, Mathilde is the kind of person who passes for vain – in no way is Mathilde vain, but rather by turns haughty and generous. As ever, it will be the task of the happy few to look beyond misleading appearances, most especially when they come to consider Julien Sorel.

On the face of it, surely Julien is in fact the hero of the novel, just as Fabrice del Dongo is the hero of *La Chartreuse de Parme*? Julien's status as a hero seems confirmed by a passage in the *Promenades dans Rome* dealing with the recent trial of Adrien Lafargue, accused of murdering his lover. Stendhal surprisingly identifies Lafargue as a new Napoleon: 'Probably all great men will henceforth emerge from M. Lafargue's class. Napoleon formerly combined the same set of circumstances: a good education, an ardent imagination and extreme poverty' (*VI*, pp. 1079–80).

Stendhal is borrowing an idea from Alfieri that, in the nineteenth century, only the criminal classes still demonstrate the strength of character that might allow for heroism (*VI*, p. 426). Stendhal's analysis is, however, original, in a French context:

> Whereas Parisian high society appears to be losing its capacity for constant and forceful feeling, passion is emerging with frightening energy from within the petty bourgeoisie, among the young who, like M. Lafargue, have received a good education, but who are obliged to work by the absence of a fortune and made to struggle with true necessity.
>
> Freed by their need to work from the thousand little constraints imposed by polite society, from its ways of seeing and feeling that make it weak, they retain the strength of their desire because they feel strongly. (*VI*, p. 1079)

We appear to be being invited, as the happy few, to approve of a murderer in Lafargue, by way of a prelude to approving of an attempted murderer in Julien Sorel. Yet, and this is a point insufficiently remarked upon, Julien really is not up to much.

A narcissist, he produces grandiose fantasies of the self – including the ultimate nineteenth-century male fantasy that he might somehow be the new Napoleon. When these fantasies are exposed for what they are, by means of a rival narrative just as plausible, if not more so, than the one so long cherished, he becomes violent, shooting Mme de Rênal. She has consistently misidentified him as exemplifying her own qualities not only of haughtiness, but of generosity – it is possible we, as readers, suspend our critical judgement partly in order to share in her view of him. Yet haughty Julien is not a generous man.

So why did Stendhal produce such a flawed hero? In part, he did so as yet another one of his jokes. Even as all our attention as readers is taken up by Julien, we miss the unexpected emergence of Mathilde de La Mole as the novel's true central protagonist. In no way a Parisian doll, Mathilde is Alberthe in terms of her freedom of thought and speech; she is also Métilde in terms of the nobility of her sentiments. But is she, too, a narcissist?

Repeatedly taxed with vanity by mostly male critics offended by her absolute refusal to make herself subservient to Julien, Mathilde is in fact full of self-reliant pride, hence her paraphrase, already mentioned, of Corneille's Medea: 'Amidst all these perils, I still have MYSELF' (*ORC*, I, p. 645). She produces numerous fantasies of the self, just like Julien; but unlike Julien she does so with a view actually to living up to them. The most developed of these fantasies will eventually see her kiss Julien's severed head, just as Marguerite of Navarre had kissed the severed head of her lover, Mathilde's ancestor Boniface de La Mole. Mathilde generates and enacts her various fantasies, in part, because she is an aristocrat of the old school – *noblesse oblige*. But, actually, she does so more because she has a horror of allowing fear or any other constraint to limit her freedom – not just of thought and of speech, but of action. It is in this sense that she functions as the azure skies: an ideal at once aristocratic and revolutionary.

One of the paradoxes identified by Stendhal is that the French Revolutionaries, thanks to their radical conception of individual freedom and self-invention, had much more in common with sixteenth-century aristocrats of the type held out as exemplars by Mathilde than the drippy nineteenth-century aristocrats who, for the most part, together cooked up the first wave of French Romanticism. Thus, in yet another paradox, Mathilde, who presents as narcissistic, is in fact sincerely engaged with the noble task of self-invention; Julien, who presents as entirely self-begetting, is in fact insincerely engaged with the narcissistic imperative of cajoling other people to reflect back to him his fantasies of self. All he really wants is what Mathilde already has and rejects: the fawning of social rivals. It is a truly wonderful novel.

It is so wonderful, in fact, that the schematic outline I have just given, of course, in no way does it justice, for it is, above all else, exemplary in its demonstration of Stendhal's negative capability. Almost nothing can be said about the novel without finally reducing it. And this is what Angela, Métilde and Alberthe all taught him: that we should never reduce people in our head, or at least not if we hope to write well. Julien is not just a narcissist; Mathilde is not just self-begetting; Mme de Renal is not just generous. The infinite play between empathy and narcissism that had characterized Stendhal's relationships with Angela, Métilde and Alberthe left him in a state of both knowing and not knowing: at a very fine level of detail, he knew everything that had passed between himself and these women, and he had many times either read their thoughts or extracted revelations from them; and yet he never lost sight of the fact that he had not, in fact, managed to find out if any of the three had loved him. In one sense, the issue is whether love in fact exists: *De l'Amour* suggests perhaps not, its being defined as a delusion. In another sense, the issue is whether sincerity is possible between two people: all of Stendhal's writing suggests it is, albeit fleetingly so. Baudelaire, a post-Romantic, understood vast amounts about

Stendhal, and yet finally nothing, for Stendhal was himself at once the first French post-Romantic and France's most psychologically astute Romantic. For Baudelaire, narcissism is narcissism and the best one can hope to do is acknowledge it in oneself; empathy is always, finally, a delusion. For Stendhal, narcissism and empathy co-exist: we are all at once con artists and our own marks, but sometimes magnificently so, in ways that allow for moments of genuine and electrifying communication – sincerity.

The writing of *Le Rouge et le Noir* started in earnest in January 1830; by the time of the Revolution in July, Stendhal was already correcting the proofs – publication was in fact delayed because the typesetters took to the streets to man the barricades. Stendhal was a quick worker when he set his mind to it, as the eventual miracle of *La Chartreuse de Parme*, composed in a mere 53 days, was to demonstrate. Around the time he was writing *Le Rouge et le Noir*, he also produced his two finest short stories, *Mina de Vanghel* and *Vanina Vanini*, as well as two not-so-fine short stories, *Le Coffre et le revenant* (The Coffer and the Ghost, 1830) and *Le Philtre* (The Philtre, 1830). He also fell in love, yet again, though this would, mercifully, be for the final time, some short-lived infatuations notwithstanding.

Stendhal had first met Giulia Rinieri de' Rocchi on 3 February 1827, while still trying to get over his rejection at the hands of Clémentine Curial. Giulia was 25 and the 'niece' of Daniello Berlinghieri, the Grand Duchy of Tuscany's recently arrived representative in Paris – he was in fact her mother's former lover.

Stendhal had immediately liked Giulia: she was young, she was beautiful, she spoke Italian, she was from Siena, hence his various references to her as 'Sienne'. But there matters had rested until 9 January 1830, when the two of them renewed their acquaintance: '*I see* Sien[ne]' (*oc*, ii, p. 118). On 21 January she was really very warm to him: 'Astonishing reception by Si[enne]' (*oi*, ii, p. 120). On 23 January he turned 47, and she was extremely kind to him:

'*Never so* bonne. *How to explain such kindness?*' (*oc*, II, p. 121). By 27 January, he had decided he was in love with her: '*Five days after, the 27: I l[ove] you*' (*oc*, II, p. 121). And then on 3 February something absolutely extraordinary happened:

Love
A singular declaration of love observed on *the third Feb[ruary] 1830*.
Right in front of him, holding his head in her hands:
'I've known perfectly well for some time now that you're old and ugly.'
And thereupon *kissing him*. (*oi*, II, pp. 125–6)

Once again, Stendhal reports the event in the third person as a way of re-establishing the intimacy of the moment. By the age of 47, Stendhal, never a handsome man, was physically an overweight wreck. On the plus side, he could sense himself that he had never been so eloquent and witty, not because his brain was working any faster, but because finally he had let go of the anxiety and the oddity and simply did not care at all anymore how he came across. People could either take him or leave him: Giulia, in the process offering eloquent testimony to the attractiveness of Stendhal's mind and conversation, decided to take him.

She turned out to be a wonderful, warm woman: kind and sincere and very aware of Stendhal's own qualities, so often obscure to his fellow human beings on account of the distancing wit, particularly when this took the form of apparent cynicism. They became lovers but also, in fact much more importantly, lasting friends.

The 1830 Revolution came as no surprise to Stendhal: Julien and Mathilde take its coming for granted in pages of *Le Rouge et le Noir* written prior to the event. Nonetheless, he was moved – as he looked down from Giulia's window on 29 July, for she was in need of reassurance – at the spectacle of workers and students rushing to sweep Charles X, Louis XVIII's senescently reactionary younger

Gaetano Ricasoli(?), *Giulia Rinieri de' Rocchi, c.* 1831.

brother, from power. Stendhal was probably glad at this point that he had not gone to the trouble of assassinating Louis XVIII: the Bourbons had done a pretty good job of ending their Restoration all on their own. On 30 July he saw a French tricolour in the street; a day later, the Bourbons were gone forever.

Astonishingly, the 72-year-old La Fayette now popped up to play a decisive role in ushering France not towards a republic but rather towards a new liberal monarchy. Stendhal was not impressed by this evident conning of the French people, and La Fayette would himself come to regret, over the course of the remaining four years of his life, the part he had played in bringing Louis-Philippe, the head of the long-liberal House of Orléans, onto the throne. This turn of events did, however, present notable advantages to Stendhal. He was now, once again, potentially employable by the French state, in search of new cadres to replace the various Ultras who had prospered in the dog days of the Restoration. Having wasted no time mobilizing his various contacts, on 3 August Stendhal secured an audience with François Guizot, who had just been appointed Minister of the Interior. Stendhal asked to be made the prefect of a French department, but far too much time had elapsed for him simply to pick up where he had left off in 1814. A politician, Guizot went through the motions of considering the request before letting Stendhal know on 11 August, via Mareste, that it had been declined. It made sense at this point for Stendhal to try to capitalize on his status as a self-proclaimed expert in Italian affairs. On 25 August, he therefore petitioned Mathieu Molé, the foreign minister, to be nominated either consul – helpfully, he suggested Naples, Genoa and Leghorn, in declining order of prestige, as possible destinations – or First Secretary to the embassy in Rome. On 7 September he received a splendid reply ruling nothing in and nothing out; he then had no option but to wait.

Stendhal was possessed of childish optimism: he had an irrepressible capacity for wishful thinking, which also explains his Romanticism – that is, his conviction that it is possible to make meaningful connections with other human beings, even though he could see, rationally, that most human beings are hermetically sealed by their narcissism. Good stuff was about to happen: surely his friends were now going to look after him, having learnt over many years to see through his oddity and appreciate his many very real talents and qualities. On 18 September he considered his chances to be 'superb' (*CG*, III, p. 778). By 23 September he felt certain he would obtain Leghorn – the lowest target on his wish list but still. On 25 September he was indeed nominated consul, to Trieste. Stendhal was delighted. He was going to get 15,000 francs a year for living in Italy – and not too far away from Venice.

On 13 November *Le Rouge et le Noir*, published by Alphonse Levavasseur, was announced in the press. Stendhal moved from publisher to publisher in the course of his career, initially paying Firmin Didot to bring out his books. His first modest financial success was *Rome, Naples et Florence*, which generated some 150 francs in royalties from Adrien Egron, as well as an advance of 1,000 francs from Delaunay for the expanded second edition of 1826. Delaunay would go on to offer 1,500 francs for the *Promenades dans Rome*. In the meantime, Urbain Canel had paid 1,000 francs for *Armance*. *Le Rouge et le Noir* earned Stendhal 1,500 francs from Levavasseur and *La Chartreuse de Parme* 2,500 francs from Ambroise Dupont, who had already paid 1,560 francs for the *Mémoires d'un touriste*. Shortly before his death, Stendhal signed his most lucrative contract, which would have seen him earn 5,000 francs to produce a collection of stories for the *Revue des deux mondes* that, taken together, would correspond in length to *La Chartreuse de Parme*. By way of comparison, Victor Hugo was paid 4,000 francs for *Notre-Dame de Paris* (1831), plus an additional franc for each copy sold, with all rights returning to the author three years after publication.

Stendhal's novels were no more successful critically than they were commercially. A year before his death, he noted in his journal that 'I have no reputation in 1842' (*OI*, II, p. 423). *Armance* received three very poor reviews in France and one in Belgium. Even Stendhal's friends hated it (*CG*, III, p. 671). *Le Rouge et le Noir* and *La Chartreuse de Parme* produced more of a critical splash at the moment of publication, both receiving, at best, mixed reviews, but only a few small ripples thereafter. Goethe liked *Le Rouge et le Noir*; Balzac liked *La Chartreuse de Parme*, but mostly Stendhal's contemporaries found him obscure, cynical and irritating. Not that Stendhal cared: he knew that he had finally written a great novel, and he was back in Italy, about to resume his career. Around this time, he makes a note in Franglais to record that he is 'à tout prendre [all in all], *happy*' (*OI*, II, p. 137). What could go wrong? The French government had initiated their bureaucratic process and informed the Austrians that Henri Beyle was their nominee as consul in Trieste; the Austrians initiated their bureaucratic process and worked out that Henri Beyle was in fact Stendhal, author of numerous immoral works, including the recently published *Promenades dans Rome*.

A first effort to block Stendhal saw his passport impounded in Pavia and sent to Milan, where he followed to recover it. After some negotiations, he was allowed on his way, if nothing else to get him out of a city that had long had him on file as *persona non grata*. On 25 November 1830 he finally arrived in Trieste, staying in a hotel – apparently he blocked the toilets, causing catastrophic infrastructural damage. He took charge of his consulate: ten days later, the Austrians appeared to announce that his credentials had been refused; on 24 December he received an official letter confirming this, dated 19 December. The Austrians had completed their bureaucratic process.

Stendhal thought he would greatly enjoy the role of consul: he had been good at this kind of work before, he would be good at it again, and it would give him both pleasure and a new-found status. Under the empire he had long fantasized about a posting in Italy: finally, he had secured one, and now the Austrians were taking it away – the way they had taken Milan away from him previously. How he must have hated them. But subsequent events suggest that Stendhal would have been best served at this point by a recall to Paris, where he would doubtless have extracted different employment from a pseudo-liberal government irked to see its nominee dismissively refused by the ultra-conservative Austrians. Instead, he was nominated consul in Civitavecchia, a port in the Papal States, therefore outside the direct control of Austria. Stendhal was appalled: 'It's a terrible hole. I was forced there by a storm once, coming back from Naples. It's permanently in the grip of fever. It's less prestigious and pays less well than my current posting' (*CG*, IV, p. 20). On 17 April 1831 he arrived to take up his new post, but was made to hang around, waiting; on 25 April the Vatican, with obvious reluctance, accepted his credentials. Stendhal finally had a steady job again, which was something, but Civitavecchia really was a hole. Stendhal would consequently spend as little time as possible in the town – he would refer to it as a 'village' (*CG*, IV, p. 107). Insofar as he liked anything about it, he liked looking at the sea, the Tyrrhenian being azure, as usually are the skies above it.

8

Muddy Roads: *Lucien Leuwen*, 1831–7

Stendhal was a perverse man. When not in Paris, he pined for Italy; when in Italy, he pined for Paris. When in Civitavecchia, more understandably, he pined for most other places. 'Sun every day,' he noted mournfully on 17 April 1831: 'I've already reached the stage of praying for rain' (*CG*, IV, p. 138). So much for azure skies. It further turned out he did not at all enjoy the business of being a consul, at least not in a minor port endemically stricken by malaria. He was supposed to be overseeing the way French vessels were treated by Papal customs officials; he wanted to be conducting high diplomacy. As a result, he decided to hand over as much as possible of his work to his subordinate and to write very long and clever letters to his superiors about how they might better conduct the affairs of state. These proved to be poor decisions.

Stendhal's subordinate – the French consulate in Civitavecchia hardly abounded with subordinates for the purposes of delegation – initially struck him favourably, in the one sense that he seemed biddable. It is for this reason that he ignored his predecessor's parting advice to adopt extreme caution when dealing with Lysimaque-Mercure Caftangioglou-Tavernier, soon to become the bane of Stendhal's life. Half-French, half-Greek, Tavernier has come down to us as a kind of Mediterranean Uriah Heep. When Stendhal found him, he was performing the duties of chancellor of the consulate, but without in fact having been appointed to this post and consequently without remuneration. Stendhal eventually helped Tavernier secure this position permanently on 19 May 1834, not that this helped improve their relations. Indeed, after particularly harsh words on both sides, Stendhal accepted Tavernier's resignation on 7 June, only to find himself forced to reappoint him a week later. Clearly, a lot of Stendhal's bad temper while performing his duties related to the nature of those duties and the town where he was required to perform them, but it did not help that he henceforth found himself both stuck with, and to a large extent dependent on, a compulsive and malevolently oleaginous liar. That dependency was, of course, his own fault: had he been willing to stay in Civitavecchia and do his work assiduously, he would doubtless neither have needed Tavernier nor himself remained for long in such a lowly post. Instead, he took heroic amounts of sick leave, to some extent with the connivance of the French ambassador in Rome.

Already in the summer of 1831, he was off to Albano and Grottaferrata in search of clean air and pleasant company in the hills south of Rome; when he had had enough of that, he returned to Rome, where he behaved as though in Paris, making jokes that terrified his audience, well aware that they could get into serious trouble just by listening to the outrageous things he said. George Sand offers us the following account of visiting Avignon's Notre-Dame des Doms with Stendhal in 1833:

> In the corner, an old painted wooden Christ, life-sized and truly hideous, became for him the subject of the most incredible commentary. He had a horror for such repulsive monstrosities, prized by the people of the South, or so he said, for their barbarous ugliness and brazen nudity. He wanted to attack the image with his fists.[1]

We may judge the effect of his various outbursts when in the Papal States themselves by the slyly charming reprimand sent to him in

1832 by Louise Vernet, the wife of the director of the French Academy in Rome and, consequently, Stendhal's frequent host:

> I'll wager that you do not realize, Sir, that I am very cross
> with you. This unawareness makes you all the more culpable
> in my eyes. I want to give you the opportunity to atone for your
> misconduct by asking you to come dine with us next Sunday
> (24 June) at precisely eight o'clock. There will be a small company.
> I shall have an opportunity to set out my grievances and to take
> my leave of you for I am planning to leave Rome for some time.
> Horace and I would be very upset if you were to send your excuses.
> Do not add a further misdeed to all your others. (*CG*, IV, p. 460)

In this period, Stendhal made friends with Donato Bucci, a dealer in Etruscan vases, the wealthy Cini family in Rome and Abraham Constantin, a painter from Geneva, with whom he shared rooms near the Spanish Steps. Another favourite destination was Siena.

Giulia Rinieri, it turned out, had no interest in marrying Stendhal, marrying a cousin instead in 1833: no woman ever proved irresponsible enough to accept one of Stendhal's proposals. She did, however, want to remain in touch with him. Even as passion cooled on her side, she continued to profess deep friendship for Stendhal and, astonishingly, she appears to have been entirely sincere in doing so. If Stendhal kept going back to Siena, mildly to the interest of the Austrian-controlled police, it was in large part to meet up with her when she was visiting her hometown.

In 1832, Stendhal spent at best a third of the year in Civitavecchia; the rest of his time he divided fairly evenly between new travels around Italy and extended sojourns in Rome. He started and discontinued an autobiography, the *Souvenirs d'égotisme*; he then started and discontinued an autobiographical novel, *Une position sociale*, telling the story of a certain Roizand, secretary to the French embassy in Rome, in love with the ambassador's wife –

echoes of his feelings for Alexandrine Daru. In 1833, when once again in Rome visiting the Caetani library, he acquired copies of a job lot of manuscripts chronicling various Italian scandals of the sixteenth and seventeenth centuries. Immediately, it occurred to him that they would make for fine source material – but he was too indolent to do anything with them for the moment. Eventually, though, it occurred to him that he ought to do something productive with his time. So, in 1834, he mostly stayed put in Civitavecchia and Rome, working on a new project.

In the autumn of 1833, Stendhal had been on leave, this time in Paris. He had spent a few days staying with Clémentine Curial – it is to Stendhal's credit just how much his lovers all seemed still to like him, even after they had left him. He also caught up with another old female friend, Mme Jules Gauthier, who gave him a copy of a novel she had written, entitled *Le Lieutenant*. This he finished reading at the start of May 1834, when he finally wrote to her with his suggestions, which included that she revise the novel completely and change the title to *Leuwen, ou l'élève chassé de l'École Polytechnique* (Leuwen; or, The Student Expelled from the École Polytechnique). Helpfully, he had already started rewriting her novel for her, when he suddenly had another of his brilliant ideas: 'don't *send it to* Mme Jules but *make* of it an opus' (*OI*, II, p. 195). What better subject, when wilting under the azure skies of central Italy, than the rain of northeastern France.

Lucien Leuwen is a political novel – along with Flaubert's *L'Éducation sentimentale* (A Sentimental Education, 1869), arguably the great French political novel of the nineteenth century. In the autumn of 1833, Stendhal had met and spent some time with Clémentine Curial's disgruntled legitimist friends, nostalgic for the Bourbons and their own lost political clout; he had also witnessed at first hand the staggering lack of enthusiasm among all classes for Louis-Philippe (his decision to designate himself King of the French as opposed to King of France notwithstanding) – it turns

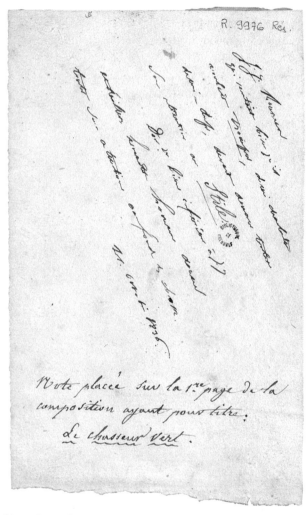

Manuscript note by Stendhal, on an unbound sheet, formerly the first page of *Le Chasseur vert* (The Green Huntsman), the first volume of *Lucien Leuwen*: 'J.-J. Rousseau, who understood perfectly well that he wished to *deceive*, half a charlatan, half a dupe, had to give his full attention to his *style*. / Dom[ini]que, far inferior to J.-J. and for that matter an honest man, gives his full attention to getting to the bottom of things. 21 October 1836' (*OI*, II, p. 283).

out you need to be popular to be a populist. It was time to write once again about the muddy roads of France.

When Napoleon fell in 1814, one of his generals, Jean Lamarque, was told by a minister in the new government that France would finally get a rest from all the turmoil of the Revolution and empire. He is said to have offered the following reply: 'That's not a rest you're talking about: it's a halt in the mud' (*OI*, II, p. 1271). Lucien alludes to this phrase when he likewise characterizes the Orleanist monarchy as 'a halt in the mud' (*OI*, II, p. 91). Orleanism, even more than the Restoration, exemplified the permanent disenchantment generated by the failure of the Revolutionary project, broadly construed. Its seeming purpose was simply to contain the anger of the working classes; its citizens lived in fear not so much of the government, which was largely impotent, but of each other, everyone having, in some way, compromised and betrayed his or her own ideals. How to earn the trust of others when one lies habitually to oneself? Muddy Orleanism exemplified 'the genius of suspicion' (*OI*, II, p. 430) that defines modernity, or what Nathalie Sarraute, after Stendhal, dubbed 'the era of suspicion', in an essay of that same title published in 1956. Stendhal is talking about the end of the Revolution's Rousseauvian dream, whether utopian or dystopian, of free citizens hiding nothing from each other, needing in fact to hide nothing from each other on account of their upholding the same universal values. It is this dream that Stendhal hopes to realize in his sincere communication with the happy few. But he is aware that most readers of *Lucien Leuwen*, as of his other works, will be suspicious of him just as he, in his turn, is suspicious of them. Luckily, they don't understand a word he's saying.

Lucien Leuwen is also an intensely personal novel. If *Une position sociale* started to tell the story of Stendhal serving as a French diplomat in Italy, *Lucien Leuwen* tells the story of Stendhal serving the empire in Germany, but with the action bathetically transplanted to Orleanist France. The first book of the novel is largely set in Nancy, but actually the 'café-hauss [sic]' that Lucien visits on the outskirts of the city is *Der grüne Jäger* (The Green Huntsman), the establishment Stendhal remembered frequenting in Brunswick, while paying his court to Mina de Griesheim in 1807 – Mina had, of course, returned to the forefront of his mind when he wrote *Mina de Vanghel* in 1829, and she would keep popping up, for example when he composed first *Tamira Wanghen* and then *Le Rose et le Vert* in 1837.

Lucien Leuwen is also, like *Armance* and *Le Rouge et le Noir* before it, a novel about high society. Lucien must make his way around first the salons of Nancy and then the salons of Paris. Almost everyone he meets is both dull and false, yet how can he ever find anything out about himself if he doesn't engage with things – and people – not as they should be, but as they are? *Lucien Leuwen*, even more than *Le Rouge et le Noir*, is a novel about surviving in the midst of relentless mediocrity.

Lucien Leuwen is also a novel about friendship. Stendhal writes often about friends, typically as very minor characters who nevertheless offer the protagonists both empathy and loyalty at key moments of distress. In the novel, the hero's friendships with Gauthier – named after Mme Jules Gauthier, but modelled on Louis-Gabriel Gros from Grenoble – and even more importantly with Coffe and with Théodelinde de Serpierre are each brought into the foreground of the text. Gauthier is necessarily a distant figure, based as he is on a much older former teacher: he is entirely admirable and therefore finally limited in a novel that shows just how well Stendhal understood that there is no such thing as 'entirely admirable' in this world pieced together out of the broken ideals of the French Revolution. Coffe and Théodelinde de Serpierre, by contrast, are Stendhal's pen portraits of his friends, both male and female.

Coffe is fair-minded, critical and instinctively envious. It is an odd combination that leads him to think very differently from, and often quite poorly of, Lucien. Not that the latter notices: it is at the moments he most reveals himself to Coffe that Lucien feels the closest to him. Stendhal provides a brilliant account of Coffe's thoughts at these times: the more closeness Lucien assumes, the greater the distance Coffe establishes in his own mind. Already, in *Le Rouge et le Noir*, we were given the story of a young man, Julien, completely isolated in his childhood and desperately eager to make connections with other human beings; but Julien had endured a hard life and, whereas he hopes for closeness from others, there is almost always a distance that he himself preserves as a means of controlling the way he's perceived: Julien is not very generous; Julien is a narcissist, at best only ever capable of fleeting moments of generosity. But Lucien has been isolated by the comfort and ease of his life – his father is a millionaire many times over. Lucien offers his friends closeness and hopes to receive it in return; he reveals himself to them and hopes to be understood; he wishes to be forgiven his good fortune, even though that good fortune has been his curse, leaving him forever in his father's shadow. The closest he comes to receiving such understanding is from Théodelinde.

Modelled on one of the daughters of Georges Cuvier, the zoologist and naturalist, to the extent that she is impossibly tall, not particularly good-looking and therefore unmarriageable by the standards of the day, Théodelinde is in fact Clémentine Curial and Giulia Rinieri, absolutely without the possibility of sex. Fascinatingly, Bathilde de Chasteller, Lucien's love interest, named after Clémentine's deceased daughter Bathilde, represents both Mina de Griesheim and Métilde, with only the faintest of possibilities of sex but absolutely without the possibility of marriage.

Théodelinde is good to Lucien, and he loves her for her goodness, almost to the point of passion, which is another way of saying that he conceives for her a passionate admiration of the type that Stendhal had conceived for Giuditta Pasta. Pasta, like Gros and Destutt de Tracy before her, had found Stendhal's esteem irksome and superfluous in some undefinable way. Did it come across as a needy invitation to reciprocate that esteem? Did it ring false, like an attempt at flattery? Stendhal never found out. But all his life, alongside a woman to love, Stendhal wanted a true friend and that friend was always most likely to be a woman. Théodelinde de Serpierre represents an effort to write that friend into existence. She does not judge, yet is endlessly perceptive. She takes everything in the spirit it is intended: 'it was with real pleasure that he talked with Mlle Théodelinde' (*ORC*, II, p. 827). She reciprocates Lucien's affection not as a way of unburdening herself of some sort of unwanted debt, but because, instinctively, she likes him and can tell what he is thinking even when he is saying nothing or saying things he doesn't mean. She is enormously relaxing: the sister Stendhal would have wanted Pauline to be, the sister he'd always wanted. 'Mlle Théodelinde was his friend [. . .]; by her side, his heart found some solace' (*OI*, II, p. 858). Thus it is that 'Lucien felt for Théodelinde a form of friendship that was almost a passion' (*OC*, II, p. 239).

Lucien Leuwen is also a novel about love. More than any other Stendhalian text, it is a novel about a man not knowing whether a woman loves him and about that woman not knowing whether that man loves her. Consolingly, both love each other; distressingly, neither will ever find out. It is a novel about all the strange thoughts we have when we are in love, and all the strange narratives we produce, and all the elation we experience, and all the devastating loss that then follows. Dominantly, the narrative is presented from Lucien's tortured perspective, but every now and again, miraculously, the perspective changes to that of the otherwise largely silent Bathilde. On some level, the latter is Henriette Gagnon, in Stendhal's patchy and largely silent recollection of her.

Lucien Leuwen is again a novel about paternity and maternity more broadly construed. Lucien is manipulated by his father, who turns out finally to be being manipulated in his turn by Lucien's mother. Both parents are finally revealed as Wizard of Oz figures: tiny people projecting much larger versions of themselves onto their son's sense of self. Stendhal is not here talking about his own father, so much less intelligent and plausible than François Leuwen, and still less his own mother, who never had the opportunity to truly make a mess of things. He is talking about power, always transparently patriarchal and sometimes obscurely matriarchal in its structures: the Leuwens wish to make decisions for their son, save him from himself, alter him, improve him. Freedom, Stendhal concludes, consists in not submitting to such power.

Finally, *Lucien Leuwen* is also a novel about empathy and narcissism. François Leuwen correctly identifies that Lucien is a dupe: that his heart is 'constant' and 'all of one piece' (ORC, II, p. 399). He therefore resolves to teach him a lesson: he bribes an ambitious married woman, Mme Grandet, with the promise of finally obtaining the political advancement she has always craved. Like Mme Roland, she hopes her husband will be appointed to high office so that she might govern in his stead. Unlike Mme Roland, she is willing to prostitute herself for this to happen. François Leuwen's object, however, is to break his son's heart into pieces, not with a view to distressing him – he is not a cruel man – but rather to educating him. Mme Grandet feigns love for a startled Lucien, who is taken in by her apparent sincerity. That sincerity is no more than a narcissistic projection: from his father's perspective, sincerity can never be anything more than a narcissistic projection. Except that he makes an exception for himself and his wife: François is sincere with Mme Leuwen and vice versa. He also understands that Lucien's own sincerity, some unconvincing moments of cynicism aside, also constitutes an exception. Ironically, at the moment when Lucien discovers how he has been mocked and betrayed and tricked, Mme Grandet is herself sincere with him – not that he notices.

Stendhal worked on *Lucien Leuwen* from May 1834 to 23
September 1835, when he abruptly abandoned the process of
revising his completed first draft, perhaps because it suddenly
occurred to him that he couldn't publish it if he also hoped to
continue serving as Louis-Philippe's consul – the novel very
plausibly directly represents Louis-Philippe as a wily old crook,
doing his best to cover up the fraudulence of his power. Why
this problem hadn't struck Stendhal before is anybody's guess.
Possibly he had been overly optimistic that the riots of 1834 would
lead quickly to the collapse of the regime. Possibly, he had decided
simply not to think about the consequences of eventual publication
– to write and be damned. What seems likely is that the new Press
Laws of September 1835, in effect reversing the gains of 1830 with
regard to freedom of expression and rendering the political
comments in the novel potentially actionable, jolted Stendhal back
to the realities of his situation. It was time to find a new project.

Immediately, he switched to the *Vie de Henry Brulard*: he was
52 now, even more overweight, hardly in the best of health. The
opening lines of the *Vie* suggest that Henry decided to pick up his
pen when he reached the milestone age of fifty: in Rome, looking
out over all those historic buildings palimpsestically representing
all the eras of the city, as a transparent metaphor for the palimpsest
of memories that will constitute the story of his life – Freud would
eventually use exactly the same metaphor for our retrospective
explorations of the self through time.[2] There's still some life in
Henry: he thinks he might have 'imprudently' (*OI*, II, p. 541) fallen
in love again, just the day before writing, during a long conversation
with the actress Amalia Bettini – it transpired that he had not.
Mostly, however, he was conscious that his life was now behind
him – hence, no doubt, his decision to have his portrait painted
in 1835, twice. One portrait was formal, the other informal.

In the formal portrait, Stendhal is shown wearing a cross –
he had received the letter naming him a chevalier in the Legion

of Honour, pleasingly in recognition of his services to literature, on 12 February 1835. It was time to establish a final record of himself. While waiting to die, he would now give himself over less to living and loving and much more to writing, to pick up once again on the activities listed in his projected epitaphs.

Stendhal wrote the *Vie de Henry Brulard* in the course of some four months, between 23 November 1835 and 26 March 1836, very much for himself, not that this has stopped the book from posthumously emerging as the most important, interesting, self-aware and formally inventive literary autobiography of the French nineteenth century. It is, of course, unfinished. After abandoning his last proper attempt to write the story of his own life, Stendhal wanted to publish another big novel, to go with *Le Rouge et le Noir*, of which he was understandably really quite proud. He also wanted to publish something that might make him some money. Finally, he wanted to leave Civitavecchia. All these various imperatives pointed towards securing another period of leave. In February 1836 he asked the new minister of foreign affairs, the historian and political rising star Adolphe Thiers, for some time off. Permission was granted on 12 March, pending the arrival of a temporary substitute. Stendhal arrived in Paris in May 1836, having been graciously accorded three months of leave. He would stay for three years, exploiting his good relations with Thiers' successor, Mathieu Molé, the man who had originally appointed him consul – Stendhal was becoming very adept at not turning up to work.

While in Paris, Stendhal tried to pick up again with Clémentine Curial, not that he got anywhere, her writing to him on 22 August that 'One cannot use ashes to restart a fire, that love had died and been buried in 1826, and that he should content himself with the status of a friend' (*CG*, V, p. 754).[3] He also tried to seduce Mme Jules Gauthier: they had, after all, already produced a child together in the form of *Lucien Leuwen*. Again, he didn't get anywhere, receiving the following rebuff, written as he stood plaintively beneath her window:

Silvestro Valeri, *Stendhal*, *c*. 1835, oil painting. This painting formerly belonged to Mérimée.

Do not regret this day, which must count as one of the finest of your life and the most glorious of mine! I feel all the calm joy of a great success: you laid excellent siege, I defended myself well, there was no surrender and no defeat, both camps emerged with glory intact. You won't deny it, in your heart of hearts there is a satisfaction that derives from what those full of doubts such as

Jean-Louis Ducis, *Stendhal*, 1835, oil painting. Stendhal is holding his favourite cane, ornamented with a gold pommel.

myself call our consciences. For my part, I am happy, and yet
I love you and to love is to want what I, your friend, wanted.
You therefore do not want what you want, and my clever instinct
has correctly guessed your virtue. Beyle, call me coarse and stupid,
a cold-hearted woman, silly, timorous, idiotic, whatever you like,
for insults will not efface the happiness of our divine conversation,

which truly honoured our hearts, our minds, elevating us to the dignity of noble sentiments. Beyle, believe me, you are a hundred thousand times better than people think, than you think yourself, and than I thought two hours ago! Adèle (*CG*, v, p. 778)

So instead he started writing the *Mémoires sur Napoléon*, his second stab at expressing himself on a subject that went beyond what could be expressed. This kept him going until the middle of 1837, when he abandoned it. He was still groping. Eventually, he hit the muddy roads of France by way of research for the *Mémoires d'un touriste*, nominally a species of diary kept by a pig-iron merchant travelling around the country. There was a market for this sort of thing, plus he could plagiarize Mérimée, who had already been

First page of the 'Egypt' manuscript, part of the corpus of the *Mémoires sur Napoléon*, as prepared by Stendhal's copyist and dated 'Brumaire [18]36' (*N*, p. 651).

appointed to his day job as inspector of monuments and who must have given him permission to lift material from his *Notes d'un voyage dans le Midi de la France* (Notes on a Journey Through the South of France, 1835), *Notes d'un voyage dans l'Ouest de la France* (Notes on a Journey Through the West of France, 1836) and *Essai sur l'architecture religieuse* (An Essay on Religious Architecture, 1837) at least, Mérimée read the *Mémoires d'un touriste* and raised absolutely no objections himself. Stendhal also plagiarized Aubin Louis Millin, the author of a *Voyage dans les départements du Midi de la France* (1807–11), who didn't give him any kind of permission to use his work, but who had safely died in 1818 and so was in no position to complain. The political judgements cast by the Tourist are all Stendhal's own, however:

> 'As for me,' the Tourist antiphrastically announces, 'I consider myself to be a very sincere friend of our King's administration and I also believe very sincerely that there's limitless corruption. I don't mind so much about the money: it's the acquired habit of swindling I mind. (*VF*, p. 211)

The fault lies, in fact, with Napoleon, for perverting the Republic:

> At the start of his reign, Bonaparte took advantage of the enthusiasm generated by the Revolution. One of his great projects was thereafter to substitute this feeling with a personal enthusiasm *for him*, along with vile self-interest. (*VF*, p. 45)

But at least Napoleon was disgusted with himself and the subjects he had corrupted, implicitly unlike Louis-Philippe, all too eager to corrupt the French people using whatever means at his disposal. The *Mémoires d'un touriste* contain Stendhal's definitive political judgement on Napoleon:

beautiful took precedence over his self-interest as a king. This was quite obvious after his coup of 18 Brumaire: often, contempt would etch itself on his fine, well-formed lips, at the sight of one of his subjects, so faithful and so obsequious, pressing forward to attend him when he appeared in the mornings at Saint-Cloud. 'This must be the price I have to pay to become emperor of the world', he seemed to be saying to himself. And so he encouraged mediocrity. Later, when he punished the generals who still had some spirit in them, Delmas, Lecourbe, etc., and the Jacobins, his sentiments were of a different order – he was afraid. (*VF*, p. 262)

This, then, is the sentimental history of the ever-muddier age Stendhal had lived through: enthusiasm had turned to servility; esteem had turned to distrust and contempt; and finally everything had turned to self-interest, suspicion and fear.

Now that he was travelling along the muddy roads of France, Stendhal also felt himself ready to write about azure skies once again, translating and commenting on some of those Italian Renaissance manuscripts he had picked up in 1833, and which he now started placing in the Paris literary press as short stories. Still he was groping, but he was about to catch hold of something solid.

9

Privileges: *La Chartreuse de Parme* and *Lamiel*, 1837–42

Among the manuscripts Stendhal had found in the Caetani library in 1833, there was a brief, salaciously libellous account of the adventurous life led by Vandozza Farnese and her nephew Alessandro Farnese, later Pope Paul III – his mother had been a Caetani. Stendhal enjoyed reading it, but initially focused his efforts on the sixteenth- and seventeenth-century manuscripts that eventually provided the raw material for the short stories *Vittoria Accoramboni* (1837), *Les Cenci* (1837) and *La Duchesse de Palliano* (1838). In 1839 he produced and published *L'Abbesse de Castro*, a much longer text set in the same period but substantially invented. Stendhal's interest in the sixteenth century, whether in Italy or in France, lay in the marked contrast he believed it was possible to establish between the priorities of that era and the timorously vile self-interest of the nineteenth century that had started in 1815. In another of his moments of genius, he suddenly understood, on 19 August 1838, that he could bring the two eras together in a single novel by framing his narrative, extremely loosely, around the Alessandro Farnese manuscript.

Manzoni had already thought of commenting on recent Italian history by writing about the seventeenth century in *I promessi sposi*. But Stendhal's project was bolder: to take a sixteenth-century (anti-)hero and his sixteenth-century (anti-)heroine aunt, and unleash both on nineteenth-century Italy. The result was, of course, *La Chartreuse de Parme*.

Fabrice del Dongo is uneducated and superstitious; he is selfish and otherwise morally vacuous; he is a narcissist, very innocently so, for he is thick-skinned to the point of complete obliviousness; above all, he is cluelessly privileged, possessing a sense of entitlement that he doesn't even understand he might be expected to question. Put another way, he is a sixteenth-century aristocrat, entirely persuaded of his freedom to do as he pleases, but also ever ready to perform the great deed that might suddenly present itself. He has absolutely no fear.

Nothing could be more Stendhalian than to have absolutely no fear. This is not to say that Fabrice is not sometimes terrified. His superstition is a function of what Stendhal refers to as his imagination. What makes Italians special is their imagination; what makes the French special is their capacity for logic, but what also defines them, for Stendhal, is what he refers to as their *a-imagination* – their startlingly complete absence of imagination. Thus Fabrice is figured as the opposite of a Frenchman:

> In his free moments, he would delight his soul by savouring the sensations produced by the invented narratives with which his imagination was always ready to furnish him. He was very far from spending his time patiently analysing the peculiarity of real events in order then to guess at their causes. Reality still struck him as something banal and muddy. (*ORC*, III, pp. 281–2)

Italians may well be amoral, nowhere more so than in the pages of *La Chartreuse de Parme*, but the French are a-imaginative.

In Stendhal's analysis, anyone capable of imagination is also capable of sudden uncontrollable terror. But there is all the difference in the world between, on the one hand, the terror produced by helplessly falling, for want of French logic, into the grip of superstition and paranoia, and on the other hand, the fear of what others might think:

What we think of as *Italian passion*, that's to say the passion that tries to satisfy itself, as opposed to *give our neighbours a magnificent idea of our person*, began in the twelfth century, when society emerged once again, and it became extinct, at least in polite company, around 1734. (*ORC*, III, p. 14)

It is then that the Spanish took over Naples, handing it to Charles I of Parma, the son of Philip V of Spain and Elisabetta Farnese, the last of her line. In *La Chartreuse de Parme*, Parma is still ruled by a Farnese, but Fabrice and Gina are in fact the novel's true condottieri, Alessandro and Vandozza Farnese respectively. Up until the Spanish takeover Stendhal is implying that Naples had functioned as the last bastion of that Italian passion merely caricatured in the late eighteenth-century Gothic melodramas of Ann Radcliffe. Thereafter, Italians learnt to talk insincerely the better to protect themselves. Sixteenth-century aristocrats, however, had yet to learn to use language to hide what they were thinking:

Vanity had yet to wrap up all human activity in an aura of affectation; it was assumed that one could only influence others by expressing oneself as clearly as possible. Around 1585, with the exception of court jesters and poets, nobody tried to curry favour by using words . . . People spoke very little and gave their full attention to whatever was said to them. (*ORC*, II, p. 994)

The paradox of *La Chartreuse de Parme*, then, is that it's the story of a narcissist largely exempt from nineteenth-century vanity, wrapped up in his narratives of self, many of them superstitious, but heedless of the narratives that others reflect back to him. Fabrice is incredibly annoying but also kind of wonderful. He's not as wonderful as his aunt, though.

Alessandro Farnese's aunt, Vandozza, allegedly prostituted herself to secure his advancement within the Church. Gina Sanseverina,

Fabrice's aunt, likewise prostitutes herself, this time to spring Fabrice from prison and so save him from being poisoned. Gina also knows no fear: she is entirely focused on her passion for Fabrice – not, in fact, biologically her nephew. One of Gina's splendid list of middle names is Isola: like Mathilde de La Mole before her, she is an island, entire unto herself, at least up until the moment when she forms the narrative that she is in love with her 'nephew'. The novel is very obviously centred around Fabrice, except that it isn't, serving in fact as Gina's story. Like Fabrice, Gina is a narcissist. This is why, in Jean Prévost's categorization of Stendhalian heroines, she is not an Amazon but a sublime harlot. Put more precisely still, Gina is Gina, Stendhal's codename for Angela Pietragrua, a sublime harlot in the manner of Lucretia Borgia.

The novel opens with a bravura chapter detailing Napoleon's entry into Milan on 15 May 1796 and the circumstances leading to Fabrice's conception, for he is as much a child of the French Revolutionary armies as he is a sixteenth-century Italian aristocrat. It goes on to provide a bravura account of the Battle of Waterloo, represented from the point of view of Fabrice, who understands nothing of what is happening around him and cannot process any of the events he witnesses. *La Chartreuse de Parme* is a brilliant novel about how we cannot make sense of what befalls us and are, in any case, endlessly in the thrall of what theoretically could befall us, but never does. At the end of the novel, Fabrice finds himself in the charterhouse of the title, ostensibly to reflect on the hitherto breathless pace of events in his life (but actually for who knows what reason): we are never told what he gets up to in his charterhouse, but it is hard to imagine his getting very far with self-analysis. Stendhal's version of Romanticism is high on impulsive deeds, whether foolish or heroic, and low on tortuous introspection.

As has already been noted, *La Chartreuse de Parme* was composed in 53 days – 52 if we consider that he appears to have taken 26 December 1838 off. The first draft of *Lucien Leuwen* had been written out in Stendhal's risibly atrocious handwriting: when he had set about revising the first seventeen chapters, he had prudently dictated the definitive version of the text to an amanuensis. He likewise prudently composed *La Chartreuse de Parme* entirely by dictating it. The opening chapter reworks bits of the *Mémoires sur Napoléon*, and there are various faint echoes of the Alessandro Farnese manuscript. But, actually, the novel represents under eight weeks of fluid, spontaneous invention drawing on decades of intelligent thought about the French, about Italians, about the Revolution, about the Empire, about the Restoration, about men, about women, about love, about passion, about narcissism, about empathy – about what it is to be free.

The novel came out in 1839. One of the first readers to appreciate its quality was none other than Balzac, who caught up with Stendhal in the street on 11 April in order to congratulate him. Touchingly, he later wrote to Stendhal in 1840 to tell him how to make *La Chartreuse de Parme* more like a Balzac novel; even more touchingly, Stendhal then had a go at making some of the suggested changes, before realizing on 9 February 1841 that he had in fact written a Stendhal novel and that he should leave well alone.

Immediately after finishing *La Chartreuse*, Stendhal went back to groping for material: would he find something else solid to catch hold of and turn into a major new work? Some not particularly interesting short stories duly emerged, but on 13 April 1839 he had another idea, this time for *Amiel*, later *Lamiel*, which was to become his fifth novel, left unfinished at his death, possibly because it was unfinishable.

On 24 June Stendhal finally had no choice but to leave Paris, and this just when he was really starting to get somewhere. It had been remembered that he was, in fact, Louis-Philippe's consul in Civitavecchia. We can guess at the extent of the enthusiasm with which he returned to his post by the time it took him to find his way back to his place of work: he resumed his duties on 10 August 1839, almost exactly three years late, his original leave theoretically having expired on 11 August 1836.

Stendhal was delayed not just by bad grace, but by bad health – gout was becoming an increasing problem. He also needed to interrupt his journey in order to catch up with Giulia Rinieri, definitively settled in Tuscany since the previous year. On 3 August Stendhal won a 'victory' in Siena (*OI*, II, p. 352) – she still loved him. One of the first things he did once back at his post was to leave, in order to spend three weeks visiting Naples with Mérimée.

Given that he was back under azure skies, it made sense to keep going with *Lamiel*. Its eponymous heroine would make great strides along the muddy roads – and across the muddy fields – of Normandy, freeing herself at every turn from the unimaginative expectations of others. Lamiel is a quite extraordinary nineteenth-century heroine: an orphan, she is entirely self-begotten in her character, running rings around those who would wish to constrain her. But then she appears to fall under the spell of a malevolent, hunchback doctor who, both usefully and patronizingly, explains things as they are to her:

'The world', Sansfin would say to her, 'is not divided between the rich and the poor, between the virtuous and the vicious, as fools believe, but simply between con artists and their marks. There's the key to explaining the nineteenth century ever since the fall of Napoleon.' (*ORC*, III, p. 1034)

Critics have fallen over themselves to assume that, from this point in the narrative on, Stendhal subordinates Lamiel to Dr Sansfin. There are many problems with this assumption. I shall list the chief of these briefly: *Lamiel* in fact has no narrative, having been left to us as a bundle of fragmentary narratives only; *Lucien Leuwen* also tells of its hero falling under the sway of a malevolent doctor only then successfully to extricate himself; it is false that Stendhal worked

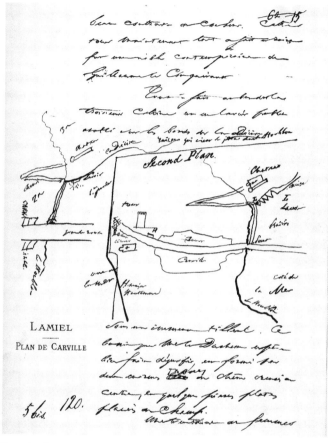

Page taken from a manuscript chapter of *Lamiel*, written and drawn in Stendhal's hand, January–February 1840. The map is of the small Norman town of Carville, where Lamiel grows up (*ORC*, III, pp. 981–2).

on a first version of *Lamiel*, in which its heroine appears radically free, only then to switch to working on a second version of the novel in which she is suddenly subordinated to a male authority figure, for, around the time of his death, Stendhal was, in fact, planning to work further on the narratives of her radical freedom.[1] Literary

The last known portrait of Stendhal, by Henri Lehmann, dated by an annotation in Stendhal's hand: 'An oasis in this desert of life. cva [Civitavecchia], 2 August 1841.'

critics have a lot more of a problem with Lamiel's freedom than Stendhal appears to have had.

Lamiel is in fact Stendhal's freest character for a simple reason: she is privileged to have no parents to try to take decisions for her. Fabrice is helped in his own freedom by his aristocratic privilege, certainly, but also by his illegitimacy, which allows him simply to cast aside the expectations of his father, visited instead on his ghastly half-brother Ascagne. But Fabrice is not an orphan; Lamiel grows up surrounded only by absurd and mercifully unrelated adults who have no authority over her and, just as importantly, no legitimate claim to such authority. Stendhal's fictional characters often wonder if they are monsters for wanting to get away from their parents, and in particular for not loving their fathers; not for nothing did Stendhal refer to his own father as the Bastard, all patriarchal power being illegitimate. But it would have been simply too easy for Lamiel to remain free had nobody ever made a convincing case for taking up a paternal role over her – Sansfin is the man sent to test her, and it is implicit in the logic of the text that she will not be found wanting.

Stendhal continued working on *Lamiel* on and off throughout 1840 and 1841 – on and off because his health was now seriously failing. Alongside his gout, he now suffered from bladder stones, migraines and high blood pressure. From time to time, his memory and even his speech would go. On 11 February 1841 he had what appears to have been a first stroke; on 15 March he had a second one, this time much more serious in its effects. It is one thing to know you are in decline; it is another to know for certain that soon you will die. In *Lucien Leuwen*, Stendhal quotes Montaigne approvingly about the need 'to grapple with necessity' (*ORC*, II, p. 369); now he noted bleakly that he had himself 'grappled with oblivion' (*CG*, VI, p. 463).

It took Stendhal a couple of weeks to recover sufficiently to have himself carted off to Rome for medical treatment and then months to recover sufficiently to take advantage of the sick leave that, understandably, he had again been granted. On 21 October 1841 Stendhal handed over the consulate to Lysimaque Tavernier. The following day, he left Civitavecchia for the last time. On 8 November he arrived in Paris, accompanied by his friend Vincenzo Salvagnoli. It took him until February 1842 to recover enough to start thinking about work. On 22 March, around seven o'clock in the evening, he was walking down rue Neuve-des-Capucines, when he had another stroke. He never recovered consciousness, dying around two o'clock in the morning the following day in his lodgings on the second floor of the Hôtel de Nantes at 78, rue Neuve-des-Petits-Champs. Stendhal had asked for a non-religious funeral, but his wishes were ignored by his executor, Romain Colomb, without whose efforts to keep Stendhal's memory and critical reputation alive, it is perfectly possible that he would have fallen into obscurity. After a brief church mass on 24 March, Stendhal was buried, unaccompanied by the priest, in the presence of three friends (*HB*, p. 443): Colomb, Constantin and Mérimée. Stendhal had specified the following in his last will and testament of 1837:

> M. Romain Colomb, who will serve as my executor, will arrange for me to be buried in the cemetery of Andilly (in the valley of Montmorency) or, if that proves too expensive, in the cemetery of Montmartre, in a prominent position, near the vaults of the Houdetot family. Above my grave, I ask M. Colomb to arrange for a plain marble slab to be placed bearing these words (and no others):
> Arrigo Beyle, Milanese
> Lived, Wrote, Loved
> Died at the age of . . . in 18 . . . (*OI*, II, p. 1006)

Andilly did prove too expensive, as did Stendhal's preferred site in Montmartre, although a lesser plot was found in the same cemetery. Stendhal was eventually moved to a better spot by the Association des Amis de Stendhal in 1962. Colomb made a mess of the inscription, reordering it as wrote, loved, lived – Stendhal, who wrote his first novel aged 44, knew that one had to live before one could write, for how else to write spontaneously in one's own voice?

Just as Julien Sorel dies in *Le Rouge et le Noir* only to be resurrected in a flashback, so Stendhal, safely buried, will now briefly come back to life via one of his most curious, moving and revealing pieces of writing. On 10 April 1840 Stendhal was in Rome, where he wrote

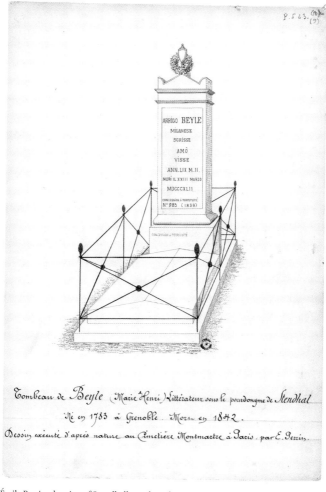

Émile Perrin, drawing of Stendhal's tomb, 19th century.

Les Privilèges, a charter granted by the God whose 'excuse is that he doesn't exist' (*HB*, p. 445) and composed of 23 articles as though in parody of the seventeen articles of the *Déclaration des droits de l'homme et du citoyen* (The Declaration of the Rights of Man and the

First of two extant manuscript pages of *Les Privilèges*, written in Stendhal's hand (*OI*, II, pp. 982–3).

Citizen) that on 26 August 1789 had sought to set men – and very conspicuously only men – free, precisely by abolishing all privileges (except for male privilege, obviously). Stendhal was one of the first people to work out that our chief human right is each to be privileged.

Just like the *Déclaration des droits de l'homme et du citoyen*, *Les Privilèges* is written very much from a male perspective, only this time with cause, for it is written from Stendhal's own perspective, privileges being by their very nature specific to the individual concerned. It is a text that, therefore, tells us a lot about the man who lived for some 59 years at the end of the eighteenth century and start of the nineteenth. A lot of the articles relate to physical well-being, reflecting his recent ill health; a lot of the articles relate to physical beauty and sexual performance, reflecting his lifelong lack of pulchritude and his inability to achieve and maintain an erection when devastated by rejection in love. A number of the articles relate to cleanliness and beauty of dress, reflecting his adult dandyism. A number of the articles relate to material comfort, reflecting his chronic discomfort after 1814. But then there are the articles that deal with his relations with other human beings.

Stendhal was an empath, remarkably sensitive to the thoughts and feelings of others. So often, he found his fellow human beings disappointing, referring to them as 'vile' or 'unspeakably base'. But then he would suddenly meet somebody whose thoughts and feelings were either consoling or thrilling to him. Article 21 would have given him the privilege of perfecting this talent:

Article 21
Twenty times a year, the beneficiary will be able to guess the thoughts of all those within twenty feet of him. 120 times a year, he will be able to see what whomsoever he pleases is currently doing; there will be a complete exception for the woman he most loves. There will also be exceptions for any filthy or disgusting actions. (*oi*, ii, p. 987)

A lot of the articles are just as careful to limit the privileges as to extend them, for the purpose of the privileges is to allow for happiness and there can be no happiness in unbridled excess. Here, the initial purpose of the article is to allow him to resolve difficult cases. Mostly, he will be able anyway to guess the thoughts of any person within 20 feet of him, but there will be times when he will be in doubt: is the person standing in front of him completely wonderful, or a narcissist set up to project a plausible simulation of complete wonderfulness? It would be good to spare oneself future agony simply by finding out one way or the other. The snooping reveals the disturbing side of empathy: as a form of violence, a trampling of boundaries. And yet one boundary must be kept in place, for the protection of the woman Stendhal most loves. Partly, this is because love must itself proceed from doubt. Stendhal was sufficiently interested in the truth to acknowledge that his love, especially for Angela, Métilde and Alberthe, might never have been anything other than his anguished uncertainty as to whether they loved him – they did not. He does not want to know, partly because he knows they did not, but partly also because some things are sacred.

That said, Stendhal had waited a lifetime for someone to give him love – mostly, he had given it himself and it had gone unrequited. It is one of Stendhal's greatest achievements as a human being that he kept coming back for more rejection. Article 4 reflects a lifetime of rejection:

Article 4
Miracle. Whenever the beneficiary wears a ring on his finger and pinches it whilst looking at a woman, that woman falls passionately in love with him, in the way that we believe Héloïse to have loved Abélard. If the ring has been slightly moistened with saliva, the woman he looks at becomes only his tender and devoted friend. Whenever he looks at a woman and removes

Second of two extant manuscript pages of *Les Privilèges*, written in Stendhal's hand (*OI*, II, pp. 983–4).

a ring from his finger, the feelings inspired as a result of the preceding privileges immediately cease. Hatred will turn to benevolence by looking at the person who hates and rubbing a ring on one's finger. These miracles can only take place four times a year in the case of passionate love, eight times a year in the case of friendship, twenty times a year in the case of making hatred cease, and fifty times a year in the case of inspiring simple benevolence. (*OI*, II, p. 983)

Stendhal desperately did not want to be alone, as he had been from the age of seven until he made his first friend, and then again when he lost that friend to death. Stendhal never recovered from losing Lambert, which is another way of saying he never recovered from losing his mother. Stendhal knows that love is illusory: it is the passion *we believe* Héloïse felt for Abélard, but that's just a fantasy that we project. And yet he also knows that love is not illusory, for he himself felt it for a sequence of women, many of whom in no way reciprocated his feelings, or else reciprocated them only insincerely, which comes to the same thing. If that love was just a state of uncertainty, then it too was a delusion, but actually, Stendhal is sure that it was more than that in his particular case: love, for Stendhal, was a function of esteem. Stendhal esteemed Angela, Métilde and Alberthe, but also Minette de Griesheim, Alexandrine Daru, Clémentine Curial and Giulia Rinieri. He also esteemed Louis-Gabriel Gros, Napoleon, Destutt de Tracy, Giuditta Pasta and a number of historical figures, most notably Mme Roland and Charlotte Corday. Some of that esteem led not to love but to the passionate admiration of friendship. The sum of Stendhal's life, from his own perspective, was composed not merely of his own actions, but of all the people he had esteemed. It is for this reason that his biography necessarily needs to serve also as a gallery containing the portraits of the people he had esteemed. Stendhal lived to understand, but also to be understood by, his friends.

He therefore hoped he would continue to live after his death,
as a result of understanding and being understood by his readers,
the happy few. For happiness to last, we have to 'dare to be sincere'
(*ORC*, I, p. 433).

10

Posterity

Stendhal predicted that he would start to be read in 1880, or maybe 1935. He thought he would come into fashion only at the point where future generations would read his work and realize that he was sincerely trying to speak with them. Most authors narcissistically project thoughts and opinions that seem to fit the expectations of their contemporary readers; how many manage to forget about all that? Not many. Stendhal determined to be one of these.

The French novelists that came after him mostly sought to rewrite, unwrite and then rewrite not him but Balzac. Stendhal was proved correct, however, in his expectation that people would start to read him in 1880. He was rediscovered, most notably by Hippolyte Taine, and then identified as the other great French Realist novelist of the first half of the nineteenth century, alongside Balzac. The problem is that Stendhal makes for an incompetent Realist: so much of what he does as an author seems extraneous to the Realist project as this has retrospectively been ascribed both to him and to Balzac. Another way of putting this is that he was a very funny kind of Realist, just as he was a very funny kind of Romantic: the privilege he claimed for himself as a writer was the privilege to exceed all easy classifications.

Twentieth-century modernism further rediscovered Stendhal. Insofar as Stendhal was rewritten and unwritten, the way that Flaubert, for example, rewrote and unwrote Balzac, he was rewritten and unwritten by Gide, but only up to a very limited point. Mostly, Stendhal has had no heirs in the same way that he had no children.

He just wasn't interested in paternity, for he cared only about freedom and happiness, which meant that he cared only about pleasing himself and his friends, and that he hoped his friends would all likewise please only themselves and their friends.

Stendhal has, however, enjoyed a posterity. The French are very proud of their great men – their great women, they often seem less sure about. Stendhal is in an imaginary Pantheon, even if his body still lies in the cemetery at Montmartre rather than in the actual Pantheon. That he evinced a certain contempt for French culture matters little to French culture. Similarly, Grenoble has long since forgiven him his jibes at the city's expense. There's a new museum in his grandfather's old flat; bars, dry cleaners and so on are named after him; the municipal library houses his manuscripts, now splendidly digitized; the university for a while bore his name and dedicated itself, in part, to researching his work. Stendhal has turned out to be a success after all. But he remains the preserve of the happy few.

Le Rouge et le Noir is widely studied in French schools, just as, bizarrely, it came widely to be set for study in the schools of the Soviet Union, Julien Sorel serving as a proto-Bolshevik if you squint at him hard enough – no, he doesn't. Schoolchildren rarely seem to appreciate being made to read *Le Rouge et le Noir*. Stendhal is a canonical author not because to read him is necessarily to appreciate his qualities; he is a canonical author because, whereas the miserable many see very little to like in his facetious cynicism or his facetious idealism – the *Edinburgh Review*, reviewing *Rome, Naples et Florence en 1817*, found his tone 'flippant', drawing a letter of protest from him (*CG*, III, p. 99) – the happy few pick up *Le Rouge et le Noir* and, after a few pages, suddenly realize it is one of the best things they have ever read: reading Stendhal makes you happy. Put another way, the happy few suddenly realize that they have made a new and lifelong friend.

References

Introduction: Readers

1 André Gide, *Oeuvres complètes*, ed. Louis Martin-Chauffier, 15 vols
   (Paris, 1932–9), vol. v, p. i.
2 André Gide, *Si le grain ne meurt* (Paris, 1955), p. 280.
3 Gustave Flaubert, Letter to M. Léon Hennique, 2–3 February 1880.
   Stendhal, for his part, remarks that 'each artist ought to see nature
   in his own particular way' (*HPI*, p. 160). 'So it is that everyone judges
   the same object from his or her perspective' (*ORC*, I, p. 85).
4 Francine Marill Albérès, *Le Naturel chez Stendhal* (Paris, 1956), p. 239.

1 Names and Identities, 1783–90

1 André Gide, *Journal*, ed. Éric Marty and Martine Sagaert, 2 vols
   (Paris, 1996–7), vol. I, p. 149.
2 John Keats, *The Complete Poetical Works and Letters of John Keats*
   (Cambridge, 1899), p. 277.
3 Friedrich Nietzsche, *Basic Writings of Nietzsche*, ed. and trans.
   Walter Kaufmann (New York, 1966), p. 700 [*Ecce Homo*].
4 Carol A. Mossman, *Politics and Narratives of Birth: Gynocolonization
   from Rousseau to Zola* (Cambridge, 1993), pp. 19–39.
5 Sigmund Freud, 'Family Romances', in *The Standard Edition
   of the Complete Psychological Works of Sigmund Freud*, ed. and
   trans. James Strachey et al., 24 vols (London, 1956–74), vol. IX,
   pp. 235–42.
6 Voltaire, *Romans*, ed. Roger Peyrefitte (Paris, 1961), p. 293.

2 Revolt, 1790–95

1 Pascale Bolognini, 'Stendhal et le secret des noix confites', *Revue d'histoire littéraire de la France*, CVII/1 (2007), pp. 215–23. We know relatively little about Stendhal's gastronomic tastes, although the *Vie de Henry Brulard* does reveal that all his life he remained peculiarly fond of spinach (*OI*, II, p. 851). This hasn't stopped Gonzague de Saint-Bris from producing *Le Goût de Stendhal* (Paris, 2014), a biographical cookbook featuring forty original recipes from the Michelin-starred chef Guy Savoy.
2 Charles Baudelaire, *Oeuvres complètes*, ed. Claude Pichois, 2 vols (Paris, 1975–6), vol. II, p. 757.

3 Truth, 1795–9

1 Pieter Geyl, *Napoleon: For and Against*, trans. Olive Renier (London, 1965), p. 32.

4 Empire, 1799–1815

1 Victor Del Litto, *La Vie intellectuelle de Stendhal* (Geneva, 1959), p. 105.
2 Stendhal, *Oeuvres completes*, ed. Ernest Abravanel and Victor Del Litto, 50 vols (Geneva, 1967–74), vol. XXXIII, p. 474 [*Journal littéraire*].
3 Friedrich Nietzsche, *Basic Writings of Nietzsche*, ed. and trans. Walter Kaufmann (New York, 1966), p. 384 [*Beyond Good and Evil*].

5 Métilde: *De l'Amour*, 1815–21

1 Simone de Beauvoir, *Le Deuxième Sexe*, 2 vols (Paris, 1949), vol. I, p. 386.

6 Restoration: *Armance*, 1821–7

1 George Sand, *Histoire de ma vie*, ed. Damien Zanone, 2 vols (Paris, 2001), vol. II, pp. 412–13.
2 Ibid., p. 413.

8 Muddy Roads: *Lucien Leuwen*, 1831–7

1 George Sand, *Histoire de ma vie*, vol. II, p. 413.
2 Sigmund Freud, *Civilization and its Discontents*, in *The Standard Edition of the Complete Psychological Works*, ed. and trans. James Strachey et al., 24 vols (London, 1956–74), vol. XXI, p. 70.
3 This fragment of Clémentine's letter was first cited in Auguste Cordier, *Stendhal raconté par ses amis and ses amies* (Paris, 1893), where the blow is softened by being given as 'content himself with the status of a best friend' (p. 38).

9 Privileges: *La Chartreuse de Parme* and *Lamiel*, 1837–42

1 See Lucy Garnier, 'La Femme comme construction dans la fiction stendhalienne', unpublished doctoral thesis, University of Oxford, 2007, especially section 3.2.

Select Bibliography

French Editions

Stendhal, *L'Âme et la musique*, ed. Suzel Esquier (Paris, 1999): *Vies de Haydn,
de Mozart et de Métastase, Vie de Rossini, Notes d'un dilettante*
—, *Chroniques pour l'Angleterre*, ed. Keith McWatters and Renée Dénier,
8 vols (Grenoble, 1980–95)
—, *Correspondence générale*, ed. Victor Del Litto et al. (Paris, 1997–9)
—, *De l'Amour*, ed. Xavier Bourdenet (Paris, 2014)
—, *D'un nouveau complot contre les industriels* (Paris, 1992)
—, *Histoire de la peinture en Italie*, ed. Victor Del Litto (Paris, 1996)
—, *Napoléon*, ed. Catherine Mariette (Paris, 1998): *Vie de Napoléon,
Mémoires sur Napoléon*
—, *Oeuvres complètes*, ed. Ernest Abravanel and Victor Del Litto, 50 vols
(Geneva, [1967–]74)
—, *Oeuvres intimes*, ed. Victor Del Litto, 2 vols (Paris, 1981–2): I: *Journal
1801–17*; II: *Journal 1818–42, Souvenirs d'égotisme, Vie de Henry Brulard*
—, *Oeuvres romanesques complètes*, ed. Yves Ansel et al., 3 vols (Paris, 2005–
13): I: *Armance, Vanina Vanini, Mina de Vanghel, Le Rouge et le Noir*, as
well as seven further short texts; II: *Une position sociale, Lucien Leuwen,
Vittoria Accoramboni, Le Rose et le Vert, Les Cenci*, as well as ten further
short texts; III: *La Duchesse de Palliano, L'Abbesse de Castro, La Chartreuse
de Parme, Trop de faveur tue, Lamiel*, as well as seven further short texts
—, *Racine et Shakespeare (1818–1825) et autres textes de théorie romantique*,
ed. Michel Crouzet (Paris, 2006)
—, *Salons*, ed. Stéphane Guégan and Martine Reid (Paris, 2002)
—, *Voyages en France*, ed. Victor Del Litto (Paris, 1992): *Mémoires d'un
touriste, Voyage en France, Voyage dans le Midi de la France*

—, *Voyages en Italie*, ed. Victor Del Litto (Paris, 1973): *Rome, Napels et Florence en 1817, L'Italie en 1818, Rome, Naples et Florence (1826), Promenades dans Rome*

—, and Abraham Constantin, *Idées italiennes sur quelques tableaux célèbres*, ed. Hélène de Jacquelot and Sandra Teroni (Paris, 2013)

English Translations

Stendhal, *The Abbess of Castro and Other Tales*, trans. C. K. Scott Moncrieff (London, 1926)

—, *Armance*, trans. C. K. Scott Moncrieff (London, 1928)

—, *The Charterhouse of Parma*, trans. C. K. Scott Moncrieff (London, 1926)

—, *The Charterhouse of Parma*, trans. John Sturrock (London, 2006)

—, *The Charterhouse of Parma*, trans. Margaret Mauldon (Oxford, 2009)

—, *Love*, trans. Gilbert and Suzanne Sale (London, 1975)

—, *Lucien Leuwen*, trans. H.L.R. Edwards (London, 1951; repr. 1991)

—, *Lucien Leuwen*, trans. Louise Varèse, 2 vols (New York, 1950; repr. 1961)

—, *On Love*, trans. Sophie Lewis (London, 2009)

—, *The Pink and the Green, followed by Mina de Vanghel*, trans. Richard Howard (London, 1988)

—, *Red and Black*, trans. Robert M. Adams (New York, 1969; rev. 2008)

—, *The Red and the Black*, trans. C. K. Scott Moncrieff (London, 1926; rev. Moya Longstaffe, Ware, 2001)

—, *The Red and the Black*, trans. Catherine Slater (Oxford, 1991)

—, *The Red and the Black*, trans. Burton Raffel (New York, 2003)

Biographies in English

Alter, Robert, *A Lion for Love: A Critical Biography of Stendhal* (Cambridge, MA, 1986)

Alter, Robert, and Carol Cosman, *Stendhal: A Biography* (London, 1980)

Brown, Andrew, *Stendhal* (London, 2010)

Keates, Jonathan, *Stendhal* (London, 1995)

Richardson, Joanna, *Stendhal* (London, 1974)

Biographies in French

Berthier, Philippe, *Stendhal* (Paris, 2010)
Cordier, Auguste, *Stendhal raconté par ses amis and ses amies* (Paris, 1893)
Crouzet, Michel, *Stendhal ou Monsieur Moi-même* (Paris, 1990)
Martineau, Henri, *Le Coeur de Stendhal*, 2 vols (Paris, 1952–3)
Mérimée, Prosper, *H. B.*, in *Carmen et treize autres nouvelles*, ed. Pierre
    Josserand (Paris, 1965)

Literary Criticism in English

Adams, Robert M., *Stendhal: Notes on a Novelist* (London, 1959)
Auerbach, Erich, *Mimesis: The Representation of Reality in Western Literature*,
    trans. Willard Trask (New York, 1957 [1946]; repr. Princeton, NJ, 2013)
Brooks, Peter, *Reading for the Plot* (New York, 1984)
Girard, René, *Deceit, Desire, and the Novel* (Baltimore, MD, 1965 [1961];
    repr. 1976)
Hemmings, F.W.J., *Stendhal: A Study of his Novels* (Oxford, 1964)
Jefferson, Ann, *Reading Realism in Stendhal* (Cambridge, 1988)
Lukács, Georg, *Studies in European Realism*, trans. Edith Bone (London,
    1950)
Manzini, Francesco, *Stendhal's Parallel Lives* (Oxford, 2004)
Pearson, Roger, *Stendhal's Violin* (Oxford, 1988)
Prendergast, Christopher, *The Order of Mimesis* (Cambridge, 1986;
    repr. 2009)

Literary Criticism in French

Ansel, Yves, Philippe Berthier and Michael Nerlich, eds, *Dictionnaire
    de Stendhal* (Paris, 2003)
Aragon, Louis, *La Lumière de Stendhal* (Paris, 1954)
Beauvoir, Simone de, 'Stendhal ou le romanesque du vrai', in *Le Deuxième
    Sexe*, 2 vols (Paris, 1949)
Berthier, Philippe, *Petit catéchisme stendhalien* (Paris, 2012)
—, *Stendhal et ses peintres italiens* (Geneva, 1977)

Blin, Georges, *Stendhal et les problèmes du roman* (Paris, 1954; repr. 1990)

Bourdenet, Xavier, '"Ô dix-neuvième siècle!": Historicité du roman stendhalien', unpublished doctoral thesis, Université de la Franche-Comté, 2004

Brombert, Victor, *Stendhal et la voie oblique* (New Haven, CT, 1954)

Crouzet, Michel, *Stendhal et l'italianité* (Paris, 1982)

Del Litto, Victor, *La Vie intellectuelle de Stendhal* (Paris, 1959)

—, ed., *Stendhal sous l'œil de la presse contemporaine* (Paris, 2001)

Didier, Béatrice, *Stendhal autobiographe* (Paris, 1983)

Garnier, Lucy, 'La Femme comme construction dans la fiction stendhalienne', unpublished doctoral thesis, University of Oxford, 2007

Genette, Gérard, 'Stendhal', in *Figures II* (Paris, 1969; repr. 1979)

Girard, René, *Mensonge romantique et vérité romanesque* (Paris, 1961)

Prévost, Jean, *La Création chez Stendhal* (Paris, 1951; repr. 1996)

Taine, Hippolyte, 'Stendhal (Henri Beyle)', in *Nouveaux Essais de critique et d'histoire* (Paris, 1909)

Acknowledgements

I should like to thank Lucy Garnier for her detailed comments on my first draft, as also Jess Allen, Sara-Louise Cooper, Fiona Cox, Marie Kawther Daouda, Kirstie Fairnie, Valentina Gosetti, Anne Green, Annika Mörte Alling, Emily Richardson, Richard Scholar, Ewa Szypula and Annette Volfing for reading part or all of it and laughing in the right places. Thank you also to Vivian Constantinopoulos at Reaktion for commissioning this biography and for her detailed comments at all stages of its development, as well as to Amy Salter for overseeing the proof stage with great patience and tact. This, my third book, is dedicated to my third son, Thomas, but is written also for Juliet, Jasper and Luke; for Elke; for my friends; and for my students, past, present and future.

Photo Acknowledgements

The author and the publishers wish to express their thanks to the below sources of illustrative material and/or permission to reproduce it.

ART Collection/Alamy Stock Photo: p. 43; Art Collection 2/Alamy Stock Photo: p. 138; Bibliothèque Municipale de Grenoble: p. 33 [PD.4 (637)], p. 34 [R.299 (1) Rés. (10)], p. 88 [R.299 (1) Rés. (329)), pp. 90–91 [R.299 (1) Rés. (63)], p. 93 [R.299 (1) Rés. (64)], p. 100 [N.3514 (5 mai 1810) (1)], p. 127 [PD.43 Beyle (Henri) (6)], p. 164 [R.9976 Rés. (21 Octobre 1836)], p. 174 [R.295 Rés. (1)], p. 183 [PD.43 Beyle (Henri) (11)], p. 187 [PD.43 Beyle (Henri) (9)], p. 188 [R.5896 (7) Rés. (446)], p. 191 [R.5896 (7) Rés. (448)]; Historic Images/Alamy Stock Photo: p. 67, p. 144; The History Collection/Alamy Stock Photo: p. 110; Masterpics/Alamy Stock Photo: p. 13; Musée Stendhal, Grenoble: p. 8 [MST.830], p. 30 [MST.41], p. 36 [MST.24], p. 37 [MST.23], p. 58 [MST.65], p. 61 [MST.1158], p. 71 [MST.214], p. 95 [MST.208], p. 96 [MST.290], p.99 [MST.294], p. 115 [MST.622], p. 115 [MST.622], p. 119 [MST.446], p. 136 [MST.626], p. 141 [MST.637], pp. 146–7 [MST.1155], p. 155 [M.684], p. 172 [M.827], p. 173 [M.828], p. 184 [MST.836].